CHINESE AND
INDIAN ARCHITECTURE

THE GREAT AGES OF WORLD ARCHITECTURE

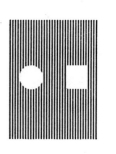

CHINESE AND INDIAN ARCHITECTURE

The City of Man, the Mountain of God,
and the Realm of the Immortals

by Nelson I. Wu
(Wu No-sun)

GEORGE BRAZILLER · NEW YORK · 1963

Library of Congress Catalog Card Number: 63-7513

Printed in the Netherlands

First Printing

To
Mulien and Ming, Ting, Ping, Ying;
my partners in building
the Gardens of YENLING YEYUAN
in the hope that we can be
Once Returners together before
becoming No Returners

CONTENTS

INTRODUCTION

The vast land of continental Asia as seen from the embracing waters of the Pacific and Indian Oceans is divided by the Himalayas into two major areas of cultural influence. Like two poignant air currents, countering and blending with each other in a stormy atmosphere, the Chinese and Indian traditions affect a large surface of the continent and nearby islands,

leaving very few pockets of vacuum between. Today, both traditions are going through fundamental transformations that are probably as significant as any in their entire histories. If architecture is to continue to provide a valid setting for, and to participate in, the new cultural programs, new forms must come forth which will echo the difficult adjustments now being made deep within the very fibers of these cultures—the religious life of India and the family life and social organization of China. The superficial architectural continuity, on the other hand, as seen in such details as the upturned eave lines and stupa motifs on numerous contemporary buildings in China and India, is no solution and brings no rebirth.

Before the next turn of events obliterates the message in these ancient architectures, we should search for the essential meaning behind the true achievements of these two glorious traditions. Different as they are from each other, the traditional Chinese and Indian architectures both refer to programs deeply rooted in everyday life, and are responsible to a collective awareness and need. Both traditions exhibit a strong desire to relate a cosmic ideal with man's own image and role within it. Only in exceptional cases, such as Chinese garden design, was the architecture ever an expression of an individual's artistic whim.

Several additional factors make it profitable to discuss these two traditions in relation to each other. For instance, both India and China, in addition to their architectural remains, have preserved quantities of literature dealing not so much with architecture itself, as with rituals, symbolism, and life in general as it involves architecture. In these writings the popular practices since primeval times and folk beliefs from various components of the nation are no doubt idealized and codified. After tumultuous eras of cultural change, periods of chaos, reunification, or foreign domination, the surviving cultural elements would close ranks and the tradition would take inventory. With all the best intentions, writers in periods of new stability incline to develop a classic-complex—a tendency to glorify old virtues, imaginatively re-creating and stream-lining details to enrich the meaning and the form of the old architecture. Han (206 B.C.–220 A.D.) and T'ang (618–906) dynasties of China, as well as Maurya (ca. 322–185 B.C.) and particularly Gupta (ca. 320–600 A.D.) periods of India, are such classical eras. The often illogical but nevertheless understandable primitive concepts and moral doctrines were frequently clouded by the confusing issues raised in these writings. They standard-ized free and organic arrangements into schemes and added splendor to architecture and rituals, but in doing so they blocked the common people's direct approach to meaning and transformed that knowledge into a sacred professional privilege of the clergy. Indian philosophers have long recognized the fact that this process of glorifying simple universal truth can create quantity (and we may add, refinement), but "more" in the end can be less than "less."

Thus,

"Unity is the imperishable; plurality is the perishable," (*ekatvam aksaram, nānātvam ksaram*); that is, the world of plurality is [not unreal, or false, but] finite, and rests on the basis of a greater, more fundamental unity, which is not finite but eternal.[1]

In both Chinese and Indian traditions, beyond their classical modes and subsequent refinement, lie the integrity and beauty of a noble primitive excitement—sense of space and sincere longing to anchor man in his universe which is eternal and immensely orderly.

A descriptive coverage of the splendor of this architecture is, therefore, not the aim of this short interpretative essay—500 or so surviving temples out of an original 7,000 in Bhuvaneswar alone, according to the 17th edition of John Murray's *Handbook*, prohibit it. Furthermore, not all important buildings in India interest us. Since Vedic times there has been a lack of ethnical homogeneity in India; in the *Rg-veda* (vii, 21, 5) there were the natives who had the phallus as their god (Śiśna-deva) and the Aryan conquerors who despised them. From this diversified origin a dynamic cultural evolution sprang up. The Islamic tradition, on the other hand, had its beginning outside of India. Thus the Taj Mahal is too foreign to be included here and too important to be treated as an elegant anecdote.

1 THE SQUARE AND THE CIRCLE

Colonized by Indian and Chinese architecture, Asia is divided into a Chinese world of walled cities and an Indian world of holy places.[2] From Java to Japan the landscape is shaped by the Chinese ideal of regulated harmony in society and by the Indian concern for eternity. In the epic *Mahābhārata* we read about the Pandava brothers who, having lost their kingdom in a dice game, revealed the otherwise vague geography of the Indian sub-continent by their travels from holy place to holy place, thereby illuminating the dark forest interiors by their visits to the hermits living inside them. At the end of the great epic, after the heroic battles had been fought and won, the victorious leader, Yudhiṣṭhira, having settled his affairs on earth, began his long pilgrimage up the Himalaya to face his God. All his experiences on earth had been but the introduction to this more important phase of his career: the climbing of the Mountain of God to receive the revelation of the meaning or truth in life. Conversely, showing little involvement with what may be inferred as supernatural will, the Chinese drama of life has its roots in the human intellect. Its dilemma is created by situations involving social institutions: loyalty, filial piety, duty, or honesty; success and frustration in the arena of man; pleasure and discomfort of the senses; and the joy of intellectual self-awareness.

Just as these value systems created by them simultaneously form and imprison the Indian and the Chinese, architectural spaces do the same. To locate man in his own spatial concept, we may discuss two basic designs which should be read as cosmic diagrams. Created collectively and hardened into a fairly rigid form through generations, they are the givers of architectural form. Inside these seeds the lush foliage and growing boughs of city or temple architecture lie dormant.

The design of the Han dynasty tile (plate 1) was not a sudden discovery. Early awareness of the rectangular shape and its orientation was clearly seen in late Shang dynasty tombs (ca. twelfth-eleventh centuries B.C.) (plate 108). In the Han image, the world of man is a clearing marked off from the unknown on all four sides by symbols in animal form. Reading these signs in a clockwise manner and oriented to the south, there is first the

Blue Dragon of the East, which stands for the blue-green color of vegetation and represents the "element" of wood and the up-reaching tree. Occupying the direction of the rising sun, it is also the symbol of spring. To the south is the Red Phoenix of summer and of fire at the zenith. Next there is the west and the White Tiger of the metallic autumn, symbolic of weapons, war, executions, and harvest; of fruitful conclusion and the calmness of twilight, of memory and regret, and unalterable past mistakes. It is the end of the road, but not the end of the cycle, for the new beginning will have to come from the all-inclusive darkness of winter. Its position is the cold region of the north; its color, black, and its element, water. There time is immeasurable and elastic. Pictured here is Hsüan-wu, a snake coiling around a turtle, two hibernating reptiles forming a picture behind man's back of life preserved underground.[3]

Facing south, his feet firmly on the fifth element, the earth, is man. Via a negative approach—not knowing how high is up, how deep is down, and how far away is the end of the world in each direction—man fixes his position as equidistant from the end of the universe on all sides, and places himself squarely in the middle. He is not represented by any picture, but his desire is expressed clearly in the abstract form of writing. Scattered inside the square world of man are these words: "One thousand autumns and ten thousand years, enduring happiness, never to end!"[4] Hundreds of designs similar to this one are found on tiles and bricks from Han sites—self-portraits of the houses or cities of which the tiles were a part.

The Amarāvati medallion (plate 2), unlike the Han tile, is unique. But there are numerous similar compositions and even more numerous spontaneous designs throughout all ages formed by Indian people weaving themselves in dances, festivities, and pilgrimages (plate 6). In this medallion, man has *evacuated* the center and is adorning the object of worship. If we should manage to untangle the figures and set them on their feet, most of them would not be able to support themselves. Yet when Buddhism calls the tune these figures of unlikely anatomy are alive, lithe, and light on their dancing feet. This picture can be expanded indefinitely by adding more circles of believers who collectively define the center of their universe.

The medallion is identified as illustrating the translation of Buddha's Alms Bowl to the Tushita Heaven, where "it was to be worshipped by all the devas with flowers and incense for seven days, and Maitreya Bodhisattva the next Buddha, on seeing it would explain with a sigh, 'the Alms Bowl of Sakyamuni has come.' After this it returns to India where a sea-dragon, or Naga, takes it to his palace till Maitreya is about to assume Buddhahood, when it will finally be conveyed to him by the four heavenly kings, Dhatarashtra, Virudhaka, Virūpākṣa and Vaisravana, who preside over the four quarters and who first presented it to Sakyamuni."[5] Connecting the scenes in these different worlds is the central image, here a bowl, but in other instances a tree, a stone, a serpent, or an anthropomorphic god traveling up and down the eternal shaft of time. However numerous, the surrounding figures always play a role subsidiary to the central image.

Furthermore, both the medallion and the tile have a third dimension. The "center" of the medallion is somewhere about halfway between the middle and the top. It is where one would expect to find the North Pole on the picture of an axially tilted globe, and the rings of dancers are analogous to its latitudinal lines. It suggests the all-inclusive shape of a sphere but with the invisible half concealed from man's knowledge. Foreground figures are seen in full, while only the heads of those in the distance are visible. Running through the center is the path of the alms bowl through the layers of heavens. The infinite universe of India revolves around that cosmic axis. On the other hand, the Chinese universe is actually a cube. The design here is merely a plan of it. The central shaft is memory, that tenacious tie of ancestral worship, and is also time. In *Huai-nan Tzu*, a Han dynasty book almost contemporary with the making of this type of tile, the reality of the universe is understood as the combination of "a six-sided world" (top, bottom and four sides) plus "past, present, and future."[6] As this cube of a universe spins down the central axis of time, Chinese history unreels, the four seasons revolving with the Chinese cyclical calendar. There are good years and bad years, but the nation is forever the Central Kingdom.

With great naïveté and ease, the ancient Chinese and Indian artists translated volume into two-dimensional design, and put time in the structure of composition; this and the other worlds became geometrically related. Human beings ritually or ceremonially involved themselves in these spaces. Throughout the ages, their architectures reveal their fascination with this spatial experience.

13

2 THE INDIAN MOUNTAIN OF GOD

A discussion of Indian ceremonial architecture is easy to begin, because it begins with any object of worship in any place. A small mound of sand made between the two hands of a brahmin on the holy shore of Dhanushkodi (plate 4) is just as valid an example as the stone cylinder known as a linga in any small roadside shrine, or the towering edifice of the Temple Lingarāja (plate 54) that rivals medieval Christian cathedrals in Europe or pre-Columbian temples in Central America.

Perhaps since the earliest times two basic notions have been behind the Indian concept of architectural space. The *void*, such as an area enclosed by a system of balustrades or walls, or its sculptural version the yoni, indicates the intense concentration of emotion for worship, in contrast to the uncommitted space outside. The *solid*, on the other hand, serves as a focus of worship, taking the form of, for example, the linga, the altar, the column, or the stupa. The column, especially when surrounded by a balustrade, makes a good example of these notions translated into stone. King Aśoka of the Mauryan Empire (ca. 322–185 B.C.), a patron of Buddhism, erected many columns of Persepolitan vintage (plate 5; for other balustrades and columns, see details in plates 9, 23, 89). Standing alone as a monument, the column was no longer the weight-bearing member of a Persian palace but became an Indian religious art motif. Its uncompromising shape, polished surface, and great height distinguished it from the natural forms around it, making it a religious signpost. Any symbol of Buddhism, such as a lion, a bull, or the Wheel of Law, may form its capital; but all should be regarded as visual aids for the contemplation of the formless truth that is supposed to be beyond them all.[7] As such, these columns occupy an important intermediate position between the simplest cosmic diagram and the sophisticated stupas and temples in the architectural tradition.

Three basic architectural types from the Buddhist tradition, all available for study today, form the basic vocabulary of the monastic complex. They are the vihara, the chaitya, and the

14

stupa; referring respectively to a monastery cell group, a hall of worship, and a relic mound. The term vihara, literally the pleasure garden of a monastic precinct, has come to denote the dormitory and hall combination (plates 8, 10, 12).[8] Many rock-cut examples, Buddhist, Hindu, or Jain are in good preservation today. While in use, the religious mountain retreat, complete with excavated water reservoirs in the living rock, was measurable by its viharas. Each small rectangular cell, half filled by a stone berth some two by six feet along one wall, was the space for one monk. When the monsoon rain swept across the plain, and the field as far as one could see was green, the monks returning from their alms-begging, religious functions, and travels, repaired to their vihara, to the comfort of simplicity and the depths of Mother Earth.

An interesting early case of borrowing or sharing between different Indian religions can still be seen in the entrance to a first century B.C. vihara at Bhājā, not far from Bombay in the Western Ghats. Two great Hindu gods, the Sun God, Sūrya, and the Rain God, Indra, are here guarding the doorway for a younger religious order, Buddhism. The Sun God journeying across the sky in his chariot supported by the billowing clouds balances the Rain God placed on the other side of the doorway, thus creating within the framework of contrast a celestial harmony (plates 7, 9). There is plenty of evidence that Hinduism borrowed back from Buddhism later in the Gupta period. Innumerable ways of blending in a three-way exchange (including Jain) of architectural technique, of symbolism, and perhaps of the masons themselves, became routine.

One of the earliest rock-cut chaityas is also at Bhājā (plate 16). It contains a stupa at the apsidal end deep in the excavated cave and a row of columns along each side, dividing the main space into what may be described as a nave and two side aisles. This simple interior space comes to life when animated by man in the rite of circumambulation (*pradaksiṇa*), the ingenious age-honored practice of translating a path in the space of our world into a religious experience. The ancient text of the *Śatapatha-Brāhmaṇa* prescribes such a trip to the unknown and back, telling how the priest first

15

> ...moves thrice round from right to left [facing the altar, first right then left, thus counterclockwise], spreading the sacrificial grass all over the altar; ...he reserves as much as may serve for the *prastara*-bunch. He then moves again thrice round the altar

from left to right [clockwise]. The reason... is that, while the first time he went away from here after those three ancestors of his, he now comes back again from them to this, his own world.[9]

Circumambulation became a complicated affair in later Buddhism with the monks chanting the sutra while tracing a labyrinth of a mysterious winding path, known as *ch'uan-hua* (weaving a flowery pattern), as part of elaborate services in Buddhist temples of China.[10]

To a devout pilgrim, a visit to a famous chaitya-hall must have been indeed like a trip into another world (plates 12–19). Having come from perhaps hundreds of miles away to arrive finally at the foot of the hill, he followed the footsteps of other pilgrims winding their way up, wearing the special paraphernalia of the pilgrim, not knowing exactly where the cave would be found but already excited by the proximity of it. At the entrance, he responded to the awe and anticipation of entering a cave. Further conditioned by religious rituals, the pilgrim stepped in.[11]

He probably would have entered from the left and thus would naturally circumambulate the stupa toward the right (a clockwise pattern). At first, he might still have been able to measure depth by counting columns as he passed them; but later, step after cautious step, his penetration into the unknown would be gauged by the dimmer and dimmer light reflected from each column that glided quietly to him from darkness. Suddenly, between the columns, he made out the spherical shape of brightness, the dome of the stupa, which glowed in the light from the opening of the chaitya—a well-calculated effect. The intercolumniations were approximately the same; but his angle of view of the stupa in between columns increased with each step he took. When he was nearest the stupa, the maximum width of his field of vision, combined with his closeness to it, made the focus of worship almost too powerful to behold (plate 19). Although we have no idea how anyone in his particular hierarchical position should circumambulate the stupa—in the ambulatory, in the nave, once or three times,[12] it is plain that the architectural space was made for physical involvement. In a cave like this, entirely carved out of the living rock, the predominant thought was that here, inside the womb of the earth, one was to seek an encounter with the very seed of the power-giving nature of religion, circumambulating the cosmic axis inside the mountain itself. Of course the penetration of some 50 or 60 feet (or in the cases of Kārlī and Kaṇherī, measuring from the remains of superstructure or entrance steps, some 150 feet) was less than skin-deep in relation to the size of the mountain (plate 15). But the darkness of the cave helped to arrest time, and as depth was measured by steps and the metabolism of the person involved, the short distance of intense and accelerated excitement could be translated into a deep penetration of earth (plates 13, 17, 18).

An earlier experience of the cave is illustrated by a group of excavations dated in the third century B.C. in the Barābar Hills some sixteen miles north of Gaya in Bihar. The so-called Lomas Rishi Cave (plates 11, 14) has its entrance at a 90-degree angle with the axis of the chamber to the left. The interior is extremely dark, but because of the level floor and the mirror smoothness of the polished stone surface, it is also hospitable and kind. The rectangular chamber ends in another entrance, this time to a circular inner room with a mushroom-shaped broad overhang and a sensuously thick wall which almost implies flesh. The circular "building" inside the cave invades the rectangular chamber by pushing itself in along the central axis. Both spaces, walled in by surfaces that absorb no sound whatsoever, rumble forever, echoing the most inwardly released murmur. This element of sound, once experienced by the first dwellers of caves, must have remained in the minds of the designers. The countryside of Barābar Hills still preserves a very ancient image (plate 3). The haystack seen in that part of India today is of course no chamber, but its proportion, its overhang, and even its softness, are all there in stone in the Lomas Rishi Cave.

In the open, the stupa has a different relationship with its surroundings. As a pilgrim approaches the hill on which the stupa stands, as in the case of the Great Stupa (Stupa I) of Sanchi, the silhouette of the structure against the sky, and particularly the central mast (yaṣṭi), will immediately attract his attention. This view at a distance, its strong general statements completely free of details and refinements, may be compared with the religious experience of accepting the fundamental commandments before the rituals and the practice of the vows create issues out of them. It is the primary revelation of truth to be followed by agonizing paths in which one loses sight of it until the time of final salvation. The pilgrimage to a stupa is thus different from the visit to a chaitya; the latter is a brief isolated hibernation from life, the former a reassuring culmination of a conscious effort.

The three stupas now standing on the hills of Sanchi were built over a period of approximately two hundred years, from the

17

second century B.C. to the first century A.D.[13] With the other buildings gone, all three heavily restored stupas are plainly visible, as if they were in the same museum gallery. When approached from an ancient path on the west, the old Stupa *II* is the lone occupant of its site, seizing the attention of the visitor as it rises suddenly in front of him (plates 20, 22). Stupa *III* (plate 21), somewhat younger, is on the opposite slope of the site and may be approached from a different direction. The present Stupa *I* is the youngest, but it occupies the site where the oldest original stupa once stood, naturally the highest point of the plateau. Like a Gothic cathedral visible from miles away, it dominates the landscape, as the original stupa must have done before it.

The circumambulation of Stupa *II* is simple and clear. The gateways are so constructed that they turn the visitor to the left as he enters and immediately prescribe a right-hand pattern of circumambulation. If coming to the stupa has been a rational act of free will on the part of the pilgrim, he surrenders to the architectural space once he is on the path inside. The ritual has taken over.

The entrances to Stupa *I* have elaborately carved gateways (torana) over them (plates 23, 24). As one approaches, the torana will rise to frame and control the view, while the *yaṣti* that has so far guided him disappears completely from sight. The pilgrim will then be occupied with the details of the carving which hitherto could not be read. Within an arm's reach and at his eye level there will be the panels illustrating the miracles of Buddha. Around the corner there will be the guardians of the holy place, many borrowed from Hindu faith. The vastness of religious "knowledge" humbles the pilgrim: a scene from a Jātaka Tale here, or a pictorial summary of the life of Buddha there. He cannot be sure of his authority in such matters. However, faith will come to his rescue if knowledge fails him. He follows the path and walks on.

Reflecting a more sophisticated ritual than that practiced at Stupa *II*, the firmly controlled circumambulation space of Stupa *I*–effected by greater mass of the stupa, the addition of torana, and the higher balustrade–was probably meant to be entered from the south. Stylistically, the southern gateway's carving appears to be the oldest of the four, and its path is effectively blocked by the high base of the stairway which makes at least one circumambulation on the ground level necessary before ascending.[14]

18

Coming around the base of the stupa, the path leads to the inviting stairs near the south gate and coils tighter on its way up. The pilgrim is thus sped around faster as the circumference becomes smaller on this higher level (plates 25–27). Here the circumambulation of the fountain of religious power is performed and the climax of the pilgrimage achieved. As the coiled path loosens on its way down and out, the pilgrim will feel like a kite with the line meted out as he flies away back home; the other end of the line, still wound around the spool, will at once restrict his freedom and guarantee his stability.

Although Stupa *III* has a similar stairway, it does not have a real ground-level passageway. It seems to suggest that the entire countryside—or indeed the whole world in the symbolic sense— is a labyrinth of passageways that man must tread before he finds his way here for salvation (plate 21).

There are many elaborate and monumental stupas existing in Buddhist countries such as Burma, Thailand, and Ceylon (plate 29). The greatest and most sophisticated of them all is the eighth-century monument in central Java known today as the stupa of Barabudur; it is also the most artistically satisfying. Lost to history for a millennium, it is once again a center of pilgrimage.[15] The stupa is in a long, fertile valley, again on top of a small hill, nestling against a protective backdrop of mountains. The whole field is thus the nave of the chaitya; the hill the stupa's pedestal; and heaven above its arched ceiling. As the mist rises from the foothills of the valley, this enormous monument reveals its volatile silhouette, light as the rising crest of a wave (plate 28). It has a comfortable curvature, suggesting a basically simple geometric design, and its crushing weight is distributed effortlessly down its slopes, flowing into the supporting natural hill.[16]

Its nine levels symbolize the nine levels of the cosmic mountain, Mt. Meru, complete with a subterranean terrace where the enlightened desire to ascend begins (plates 30, 31, 32, 36, 40). From this underworld of nightmarish experiences, illustrated by the bas-reliefs, the entrapped godly nature of man distinguishes the right path from the wrong. Waiting for him above are the square terraces representing this world, and the circular terraces representing the world of God. Busy and crowded scenes of nature and of the previous lives of Buddha as told in the Jātaka Tales, palace scenes, and Buddhist scenes are carved along the narrow corridors and accompany the pilgrim as he goes around. But, as he emerges from the galleries to the circular terraces, all these are left behind. Even the walls that have channeled him are now beneath. It is an awesome experience to rise finally above all these and to see the 72 smaller stupas in concentric circles building up to a crescendo on top of the cosmic mountain. The pilgrim is no longer held inside the valley of the mountain ranges; but he is separated from the world below by his new elevation.

The smaller stupas are hollow inside. Through the perforated shell the pilgrim can see the half-hidden Buddha sitting in the meditation posture looking away at the horizon. Without the walls, he notices for the first time the movement of everything around him. The smaller stupas seem to move as he moves; now falling in line, now forming a spiral; now a complex geometric pattern that whirls around like a pinwheel, tighter in the center and more spread out on the edges (plates 37, 38). On the horizon the mountains revolve with the stupas.

At the four cardinal points are passageways going straight to the center from the first terrace. A pilgrim can catch a reassuring glimpse of the central stupa through the succession of doorways each time he completes a quarter of a circle (plate 35). Treading the right path in the Mountain of God, he knows that he is heading for the Supreme Truth even though the central stupa is so frequently out of sight. However, the gratifying feeling of arriving on the upper terraces confronts him with a confusing forest of stupas. At this darkest moment just before the enlightenment, we can almost hear a desperate cry of bewilderment, something similar to "Father, Father, why hast Thou forsaken me?" Then, there is the central stupa (plate 39). The pilgrim has joined the myriad worshipers throughout the ages dancing around the central motif.

All images, architectural structures, and the ritual passageways are but means to an end. It is in this sense that the greatest stupa of Barabudur, the enormous linga and pyramid of Tanjore, and the colossal Buddha figure at Bāmiyān function in the same manner as a small mound of sand shaped between the hands of the brahmin on the shore of Dhanushkodi (plates 4, 58, 59).

The sequence of visual and spatial experience at Barabudur goes from naturalistic sculptured images on the lower level to schematized images above, from busy surfaces to simple ones, from diverse religious scenes and passageways to the unified image—until the austere theme of the stupa is repeated seventy-two times. It is a most eloquent statement of the "perishable plurality" versus the "eternal unity," with the refrain repeated again and again after the verses have been sung.

A stupa, having a central plan, faces no particular direction; it faces all directions at all times. At Barabudur, as we have seen, the seventy-two dhyāna Buddhas face out, and together solve the problem for anthropomorphic figures of facing all directions at the same time. This solution is seen on many pagodas and freestanding monuments which symbolize a Buddhist beacon of light, with numerous small icons radiating light to illuminate all corners of the universe. In the two-dimensional design of the Buddhist mandala (cf. stupa base at Nāgārjunakoṇḍa, plates 33, 34), there is a double spatial relationship: the plan is seen from above and the figures from the front. As the Buddha faces the viewer forever, he is facing any direction from which he is seen. This problem of portraying the omnipotent religious energy is a very real one in temple architecture of an axial plan.

While the perfect form of the linga and the altar served the Hindu faith well, the challenge of the central and axial plan in Hindu temple design inspired a complete saga in architecture. The temple is at once the notion of God, the dwelling of God, the body of God, and the holy act of man utilizing tangible substance to realize all these abstract ideas. Thus its basic plan is not the abstract and eternal rimless circle, but the *vāstupuru-samaṇḍala* (Vāstu, the Site; Puruṣa, the Essence; Maṇḍala, the Form), whose manifestation is a square.[17] The development of the Hindu temple from the Gupta period to the later Hindu dynasties is a splendid effort to honor this basic and perfect form. The supporting tower motifs, when they appear, only help define the central theme; and the sequence of halls forming the approach, no matter how elaborately designed, remains a means to this end (plate 53).

The Deogarh temple is the Gupta version of the enclosed focus of worship, and it brings to conclusion the space it organizes. A nine-square plan for the temple structure, located in the center of an enclosed "void" of the temple ground, is distinguished by a raised platform, thus creating a new dimension (plates 42, 43). Continuing to explore the square motif, the cella rises as the vertical shaft from the middle square of the nine, symbolically coinciding with the axis of the universe. The corner projections already prophesy the five-tower plan of such monuments as the Angkor Wāt (plate 45), and recall the ancient design of the Mahābodhi Temple of Bodh Gayā (plate 46).

The elaborate axial plan in the later Hindu temple was also incubated in the Gupta period. Extant temples dating from that time usually have a front porch, followed by a square hall known as the mandapa which leads to the cella—thus a counterpart of the chaitya hall. Now freestanding, such as the examples at Aihole, they point to an important direction of new development, a direction impossible for a rock-cut hall to have pursued. The axis of the universe motif can now be restated on the outside in the form of a sikhara (literally meaning a mountain peak) directly above the innermost space in the form of a magnificent tower; and the exterior configuration and surfaces can now be developed.

Recalling the experience on the upper level at Sanchi, the Durgā Temple has a dramatically arranged open *pradakṣiṇa* path on an elevated platform. Here the pilgrim would have his last view around him before entering the dark chambers where all measurements and sense of position would switch to another set of references. The temple, which indeed looks like a boat from the apsidal end, symbolically ferries him away from this world to "the other shore" (plates 55, 56).[18] The innermost sanctuary known as the *garbha griha*, literally womb chamber, is unmistakably the most significant void. Within it the seed of religious energy is kept, ready to animate any being that comes to it. It is over this chamber of the man-made cave that the man-made mountain, the sikhara, rises.

Like so many other monuments, the Durgā Temple is heavily restored. Our reading of the architecture must be largely limited to the plan.[19] Unlike the continuous flow of space inside a chaitya, the interior of the Hindu temple with the front porch and the mandapa is a sequence of significant pauses and subtly manipulated cadences reaching toward a crescendo. It is precisely as expected that in later development the podium will gain height, the mandapa will gain in number, and the outward expression in the sequence of pinnacles will rush to an accelerated finale.[20] The ultimate development in this acceleration is seen in the Khajurāho group of temples, both Hindu and Jain, dating from the eighth century (for the earlier ones) to the twelfth (plate 57). The basic theme, however, has been well maintained. By superimposing the profile of Lingarāja on that of Mukteśvara it is possible to realize how enormous these temples have become after five hundred years of development in one town, Bhubaneswar in Orissa (plates 48–52, 54).

The chronological sequence in which the components of the great Lingarāja were constructed is significant. The *garbha griha*, the sikhara and adjoining mandapa (the *jagamohana*) belong to the first period of construction and are datable by inscription as before 1112.[21] The two halls farther away from the tower are of later date, each adding more depth to the great temple. Serving as a grand approach to the innermost sanctuary, the buildings on this axis are nevertheless related to the central shaft of the tower just as are the three open porches on the other sides: means to glorify the central theme. The corbeled sikhara of Orissa are usually painted white to symbolize the snow-covered peak of the mountain. They guide the pilgrim to the temple from miles away. Inside, the tower must exert great power, pulling the spirit of religious aspiration to a height exaggerated a thousand times over by the lack of visible reference in that moist darkness.

The identification of the temple with the mountain has resulted in some of the most magnificent rock-cut temples in India. The Kailāsanāth of Elūra (plates 60, 61, 63), dedicated to Śiva by Krishna I (757–83) of the Rāṣṭrakūṭa dynasty, had taken as its model the Chalukyan temple of Virūpākṣa (dedicated 740) at Paṭṭadakal (plates 62, 64), which in turn was under the influence of another Kailāsa temple, this time on the coast near Madras, at the Pallava kingdom's capital Kāñcipuram. The well-articulated massing separating the interior space-cells, the elaborate axial plan, and the blending of the different regional characteristics all pay tribute to the long genealogy and the variety of patrons. Using this to illustrate the migration of a design, we may point out that perhaps the professional masons who formed guilds, just as in medieval Europe, might in some manner have accompanied this journey that must have taken generations. It is impressive to think of the collective effort of the Indian people as one sculptor revealing from solid rock the image of the holy mountain Kailāsa, the abode of Śiva. Finally the seed has broken through the ground.

This image of the mountain is complemented by the presence of water as seen at Deogarh. Represented by their female personifications—the Ganga as identified by the makara serpent, the mystical animal, and the Jumna by the tortoise—the two great rivers issue forth from the *amlā* (*āmalaka*), the mountain peak motif above the middle of the lintel framing the doorway, the passage to the mountain cave. To make sure that the image of the holy mountain is situated in the middle, the *amlā* is placed above the center temple in the composition of five, suggesting the classical Pañcāyatana of four smaller shrines on the corners and the main temple in the middle. The arrangement and proportion must be read as a two-dimensional representation of the five structures: two front ones, one in the middle, and the two small ones representing those on the far side (plate 44). Down from the central peak the two rivers flow. This river motif, used as a format to indicate continuity in narration became quite elaborate in later temples. No less than seven bands can be seen cascading down the door jambs at Koṇāraka (compare plates 41 and 47). The serpentine path reaches out to the gateways of the compound in Cambodian monuments (plates 83–87).

The most fascinating process of elaboration has been justly lavished, however, on the plan, the *vāstupuruṣamaṇḍala*. There is a mathematical beauty in the star-shaped podium of such southern temples as the Keśava temple at Somnāthpur (plate 65) and other accordion-like walls at nearby sites of Halebīd and Belūr. The excitement of abstract volume reaches a new height in the form of an ablution pool at the eleventh-century Sūrya temple at Modhera, not far from the famous Jain temples at Mt. Ābū (plates 66–70). In front of the chiaroscuro fineness of the mandapa, exposed to the brilliant sun and the abrasive sandstorms of the Gujarāt, this tremendous form in void plays upon the theme of the terraces visible through water, all the while accompanied by the luminous reflections on the water's surface. This theme of the ephemeral and the eternal world could not have inspired a more beautiful symphony in an Indian temple. It is the visual image of the ancient saying:

> Just as, brethren, the mighty ocean deepens and slopes gradually down, hollow after hollow, not plunging by a sudden precipice,— even so, brethren, in this Norm-Discipline the training is gradual, it goes step by step, there is no sudden penetration to insight.[22]

Perhaps just as ancient a notion as the coming of water from heaven via mountain, e.g. "the Descent of the Ganges," is the idea of rejuvenating life inside the cave and being born anew with accumulated spiritual energy. The *Mahābhārata* cites numerous examples of how even the greatest of gods have to go into hibernation, reducing their size, seeking protection in the interior of some lowly substance to wait for better days.[23] The void of the interior space where such rites of accumulating religious merit take place suggests many possibilities for its external expression. One common idiom in religious art is the motif of of the serpent, an animal associated with water and hibernation. Frequently a composite animal form is employed for this purpose, and the mystical makara is the most commonly found. These notions may be behind the carving of the Sarpa Gumpha (Serpent Cave) at Udayagiri whose entrance is underneath the cobra hood of the naga motif. Nearby is the Bagh (Tiger) Gumpha (plate 72), which is entered through the wide open mouth of the beast.[24] Similar usage in separating one world from another is common in other cultures. Temple XXII in Copan, Honduras, with its serpent entrance way, and the *t'ao-t'ieh* motif of Chinese bronzes are other examples half a world apart (plate 82).[25] The Lomas Rishi Cave, mentioned before, shares with several other excavations one enormous boulder that has the appearance of a whale (plates 14, 71). The clearest image in this respect however is the Dragon Temple at Amarapura, Burma, which leaves no doubt that it has been designed as a literal representation of a dragon; but, artistically speaking, it is also the least subtle.[26]

Two opposing sections of the cycle of unending time are in the notion of transmigration of the soul. Hibernation takes place in the dark period, but all actions are conducted following the right way in the light. The right way is the same for all beings: all celestial bodies, including the greatest of them all, the sun, are observed to revolve around an imagined axis that goes through the middle of man's world and the northern star. The sun's way is the right-hand way. Independent sages of great mental capacity can wade through their "mental ford," the *mānasa-tīrtha*, whose "water is truth and metaphysical knowledge"[27] and reach salvation on the other shore. But for the common people there is always plenty of room on board the chariot of the Sun God Sūrya. Many images of the chariot have been made, from the small version at Vijayanagar to the gigantic "Black Pagoda" of Koṇāraka on the eastern seashore of Bengal (plates 73–75). When the time comes and the wheels turn and tier after tier of musicians begin to play, the lucky passengers and the myriad embracing *mithuna* couples, dissolving into eternal union, will ride out to the far end of the ocean rising and orbiting on the chariot of the sun.

In the great southern temple-cities the prescribed right path can be experienced on earth. Inside closed compounds, such as

25

that of the Great Temple of Madurai, there is always the famous "hall of a thousand columns," an outgrowth of the mandapa, perhaps having its origin in the dolmen. In fact, the roofed inner quadrangle is made of miles of galleries supported by columns and pilasters many thousands in number. Without the sacred clerical knowledge of processions, a pilgrim nevertheless could have his kinesthetic satisfaction of the ritual by following the musicians and the icons, winding his way along a prescribed path (plate 79). Brushing by the sculptured images of great heroes of the past, he would be happy to recognize, for instance, Yudhisthira and his brothers of *Mahābhārata* (see page 11, plate 76); coming to the sacred purifying pool of the Golden Lotus where Indra gathered flowers to worship Śiva,[28] he would be at home with the ablution rites. He would measure his penetration into the sacred sanctuary by the length of his passage, psychologically exaggerated by the countless turns he had made. The dimension of the temple here is thus measured horizontally, by movement, while the Orissan temples measure the nearness to God by the visual height of the sikhara.

A most interesting puzzle here concerns height. These southern temple-cities are encircled by rings of walls with towering gopuras over the doorways. They are like the mythical mountains rimming the Indian world (plate 78). James Fergusson, commenting in 1899 on the southern composition, expressed dissatisfaction over the fact that the gopuras on the outside are the tallest and that they diminish in height as they are found nearer to the center. He said:

> As an artistic design, nothing can be worse. The gateways, irregularly spaced in a great blank wall, lose half their dignity from their positions; and the bathos of their decreasing in size and elaboration, as they approach the sanctuary, is a mistake which nothing can redeem... It is altogether detestable.

26

He then suggested that the principles of design be somehow reversed.[29] If size in a mechanical sense is the message here, then the message is indeed a jumble. In fact, the spires over the sanctuaries of Śiva and his consort Pārvatī, known here as Sundareśvar and Minākṣi-devī, are the lowest of all the towers. Within the roofed compound, which should be considered as a separate reality in itself, Śiva's tower is indeed higher than his consort's for obvious reasons (plate 77). But both towers have the distinction of rising above the enclosed mysterious space, their golden pinnacles penetrating the roof to shine blazingly in the sun. Definitely not in the same category with the earthbound and plainly exposed doorways, these golden summits should not be subjected to comparison. They are "farther" away in the great "depth" of heaven (cf. the pool at Modhera, plate 70) because they are never visible to the pilgrim at any point along his winding approach to them. The gopuras encircle the void in the ancient tradition, and they function properly by being high and visible from as far as the horizon. But the golden foci of worship stay correctly out of sight, and shine in every believer's faith. That mechanical measurement is definitely not intended is also made clear in the rich experience of movement produced by this unusual architecture. Once inside the first ring of walls, all the gopuras will appear in a different relationship to the pilgrim: no longer the façades of a holy place, but towering peaks of moving waves dodging behind one another as the pilgrim progresses. The nearest gopura is always the tallest, and more distant ones wait their turn to come into view. When the pilgrim enters the roofed temple proper they all disappear together.

In the history of the temple-city architecture, the sequence of construction is again significant. The outer gopuras were the last ones added when the outer walls were built. Thus, theoretically, the temple can be infinitely expanded as could the world depicted in the Amarāvati medallion. The Nayak kings have done heroically well in this respect, as witnessed by the size of the compound, 840 x 780 feet. The reverse of this, having the highest in the center as suggested by Fergusson would make any outward expansion an anticlimax.

There was a special psychological need for an expanding architecture in seventeenth-century south India. At the end of two centuries of resistance, Vijayanagar, the Victorious City, fell in 1565 to its Mohammedan invaders. The leadership of the shrinking world of the Hindus in South India fell on the shoulders of the few princes who like the Nayaks defiantly constructed the temple-cities of Tiruvannamalai and Madurai. Here and in such southernmost temples as the one at Rameshwaram (plate 80), we see the high-water mark in the development of the horizontal accent in interior space.

Since the third century the land that is modern Cambodia has been a crossroad of Chinese and Indian influence.[30] In the twelfth and thirteenth centuries, after a long period of incubation, the Khmer culture enjoyed a brief but glorious florescence. Of the scores of important monuments, two are of extremely large dimensions and are also among the better preserved. Angkor Wāt and Bayon in Angkor Thom (plates 45, 83, 86) are near the modern village of Siemreap, where the ruins of ancient monuments still dwarf the houses of the native people in such a way that there is nothing to suggest a sense of proportion between such divergent sizes. These two major architectural accomplishments are excellent examples with which to anchor down a discussion of the enclosed sanctuary and the mountain motif.

If we examine at close range one of the many makara lintels that are so particularly characteristic of this region, we may see in the sophisticated image the long development that had preceded these complex monuments. This animal motif accentuating a doorway reminds us of the previously mentioned Bagh Cave whose entrance is in the form of the wide-open jaw (compare plates 72, 81). The lintel is but a stylized label for an entrance, here greatly elaborated. The makara has gained many heads, and its serpentine body many branches of subdivisions. The buildings are correspondingly complex. At both Angkor Wāt and Bayon the covered galleries are clearly translations of this two-dimensional lintel design into three-dimensional space. Visitors are greeted by enormous naga forms with multiple heads. All paths leading to the center are along the serpentine trunks on either side of the roadway and the stone tiled roof of the galleries suggests a scaly body (plates 83, 85, 87). Inside is a network of clearly defined interior volume where religious ceremonies take place. The circumambulation path at Angkor Wāt, as guided by the magnificent relief on the wall, is definitely in the left-hand or counterclockwise pattern (toward the land of death), for the architectural complex oriented to the west is the early twelfth-century mausoleum of Sūryavarman II dedicated to the region of death. On the eastern gallery is carved an enormous composition of the "Churning the Sea of Milk," with the serpent wound around the pestle for this act of creation. This vertical symbol coincides here with the monument of a great king. The superimposition of the King and the God is complete in the image of Bayon (plates 84, 86). The King, as the Bodhisattva Lokeśvara is portrayed numerous times, looking in all directions at the same time, omnipotent and omnipresent, letting his image be the image of the mountain that is the pestle with which the gods and "demons" churn.

If we re-evaluate the entire temple-mountain development with reference to the role of man, we will see that he is never as

28

insignificant as he at first appears to be. He must take pride in the edifice that he has caused to be erected or carved. If he believes theoretically that his achievement is but a miserable, ephemeral counterpart on earth of what is infinitely more magnificent in heaven, he must also be quite convinced of the importance of "practice" (*yoga*), and of the merit one earns by it. As he dedicates the religious edifices, his man-made mountains must measure virtuously in this era of *kaliyuga*, the fourth and the most sinful cycle of time in the great Hindu *kalpa*. Man's arrogance gives form to his inflated desire to worship and to glorify himself; his monument must endure as anything can endure. So, when water comes down from heaven and is intercepted by the head of the god-king (Devarāja) just as the braided hair of Śiva received the water of the Ganges,[31] the image of the head of state is clearly that of the agent between heaven and earth in the act of receiving and redistributing water to bring life to the rice field of the empire.

These lush countries, instinctively aware of the dynamic forces of nature, are the very places where nature reclaims the myriad human symbols so consciously developed throughout the ages, reducing them once again to become one within the great unity that is nature. A panel from the Great Stupa of Sanchi prophesied this in stone. It is an image existing only in time: a superimposed sequence of a platform or altar of worship, a balustrade enclosure, a chaitya; and from the seed inside there germinates a magnificent tree branching out and reaching up-ward, then gloriously shading all with its foliage. The same eternal image is the work of the forces of nature, here in the ruins of Angkor, as they act upon "matter" (*prakṛti*), the sub-stance of man's art (plates 88, 89).

3   THE CHINESE CITY OF MAN

The rectangular Han dynasty tile we discussed in Chapter 1 (plate 1) is a rigid, finite, and unnatural design. Wherever cir-cumstances permit, this image is readily translated into the equally unnatural classical city plan of China, sometimes using the same animal symbols to name the gates at corresponding cardinal points. It manifests an intellectual order superimposed upon a natural terrain. The T'ang dynasty capital of Ch'ang-an and its Japanese copies, Nara and Kyoto, are such expressions. This tradition, developed in the north, eventually influenced such southwestern areas as Szechwan and Yunan. Their capitals, Ch'eng-tu and Kunming, interesting variations of this basic design, make a dramatic contrast to a southeastern, naturally shaped river-town like T'ung-lu in Chekiang province (plates 90, 112, 113). This rationalized basic design is not only frequently seen in city plans but is also sensed in the layout of houses, palaces, and tombs. Always keeping man in its center, it is an image of man's society, organizing its enclosed space around him. The Chinese designer is continually challenged and inspired by the specific requirements of each social program and by the human relationships in the society which his building serves and portrays.

The engineering problems of construction or the discovery of new materials are relatively unimportant here in the generation of new ideas. For instance, the bracketing system, *tou-kung*, has not seen any fundamental change since its standardization (plate 128), and similarly, the early knowledge of the true arch never initiated a masonry tradition. The drama of Chinese architecture's struggle to meet the requirement of its program is thus one of ingenious exploration of the potentialities of the wall, the height of the platform, the placing of individual buildings, the organization of a compound. It concerns itself above all with the prescribed *position* and *movement* of man in an architectural complex. The effect thus created is sometimes unclear even to the central figure around whom an entire composition is organized.

We read of such an example in the history, *Shih Chi*. In the fifth year of Han (202 B.C.), having already unified China, the King of Han was enthroned as emperor. Scrapping all the elaborate ritual procedures of the previous dynasty, the new emperor had a simple ceremony. His officials and generals had a riotous time drinking and boasting of their part in founding the dynasty. The Grand Audience Ceremony two years later, with the help of new rituals and the architecture of the newly remodeled Ch'ang-lo Palace, was conducted in a totally new atmosphere. Throughout the day of celebration, solemnity and orderliness ruled. The feudal lords, officials, and generals arrived at daybreak and were ushered into the courtyard in front of the grand and steep terrace on which stood the audience hall.[32] Chariots, mounted guards, and foot soldiers were displayed with appropriate flags and standards. The military officials stood on the west side facing east. Civil officials from the prime minister on down lined the east side facing west. Messages to and from the emperor were conveyed by special messengers who scurried swiftly about. Hsiao Ho, the Prime Minister (also the chief architect in charge of works for this and other palaces), was granted the special dignified privilege of "walking" instead of scurrying in front of the emperor. At the ceremonial banquet the ranking nobles and officials ascended the high platform and attended the emperor. The emperor sighed, "I know only now the exalted status of the Ruler of Man!"[33]

The buildings are no longer extant, but according to the literary descriptions there were certainly bold attempts at using height, enclosure, and relationship between structures to support the intended climax. Perhaps the concern of a specific program does not encourage permanence in buildings with the result that when a new need arises, palaces and temples are frequently dismantled and used for a new purpose, sometimes at a site hundreds of miles away.[34] In addition to this, Chinese tradition calls for the use of perishable earth and wood ("*t'u-mu*"), two kinds of material that have come to mean "buildings" or "architecture." Keeping in mind, therefore, the creation, the destruction, and the decaying of Chinese buildings, we cannot regard the accidental preservation of a few tombs, pagodas, and temples as wholly typical of the architectural development. Too often a historical narration of Buddhist architecture has been substituted for a history of Chinese architecture. The lasting values in the tradition beginning with the formative period of Han (at the latest) perhaps should be sought in the enduring design that has shaped the humble family house as well as the Chinese city of man. The house is the basic cell in the organism of Chinese architecture, just as the family it houses is the microcosm of the monolithic Chinese society.

From ceramic models found in tombs, and murals of tomb chambers and temples, we have no lack of examples showing the types of houses built from Han to T'ang times. Literary documents supply information about the dwellings of much earlier date. Certain basic techniques of composing a house seem to have survived extremely well and are still found in modern

31

buildings. In one type, a few rooms are connected by walls to form a yard ("*t'ing*" or "*yüan*") utilizing the back wall of the rooms as the exterior wall of the compound. The other type, also well developed and seen frequently in T'ang dynasty murals, has freestanding buildings set within the yard requiring a continuous wall to enclose them (plates 91–93). Both clearly demonstrate the significance of the courtyard, which as a negative space plays a prominent role in forming the "house-yard" complex. The student of Chinese architecture will miss the point if he does not focus his attention on the space and the impalpable relationships between members of this complex, but, rather, fixes his eyes on the solids of the building alone.

In our sequence of photographs, using houses both in the city and the village, we hope to identify quickly the courtyard and certain other aspects of the Chinese house that deserve our special attention (plates 94–104, 107, compare plates 102, 112). The first thing to be noticed as different from a Western house may be called the separation of the roof from the wall; they do not meet at the eave line. Between the wall of the site and the eaves of the house is the courtyard. The privacy here is a partial one; horizontally the yard is separated from the street by the wall or by the surrounding buildings, but it shares both the sky and the elements of the weather with other houses and yards. As the wall blocks only the view, thus creating a visual privacy, it offers a particularly refreshing experience of communication with the outside through the senses of hearing and smell. Chinese literature abounds with examples describing city life through the sounds of the peddlers on the streets and the scent of the flowering trees coming over such a wall. The implicit paradox of a rigid boundary versus an open sky reminds us of the similar situation in the land use of this ancient agricultural country: while the boundaries of farm land are guarded by everyone, the "Will of Heaven" is a fate shared by all.

The buildings themselves provide another kind of partial privacy. Although the area underneath the protruding eaves offers man privacy from heaven or from the "Heavenly See," it opens horizontally to the yard, the area of semi-private space. By the same token, the central room (known as the *ming*, meaning bright), connecting the porch and the inner (*an*, or dark) rooms, is another intermediate space before the total privacy of an inner room either to the right or to the left. The meaning of this, if we may coin a term and call it graduated

32

privacy, can best be demonstrated by placing people in these simple basic houses as if they were chess pieces on a board. Outside the front gate is the world of strangers. A peddler may be stopped near the door or invited into the doorway to show his wares. Friends and relatives expect further invitation to the courtyard. The platform distinguishes itself from the yard vertically. On it, the porch and the *ming* room are places to receive guests. Womenfolk sometimes are required to hide themselves in their rooms.

Educated from childhood in such etiquette, the ancient Chinese learned to be at the right place at the right time and to follow the right path. The simple acts of everyday life merited attention from the *Li Chi*, the *Book of Rites*, a Han dynasty compilation from accumulated source materials of much earlier periods. The rational and the official version of what was proper behavior may be gathered from a few excerpts. As "the essence of *li* ["social norms" or, in this case, "etiquette"] is to humble oneself in order to honor others," the use of *li*, therefore, is "to assure security [under *li*, or orderliness in correct conduct]. *Li*-lessness means danger."[35] In a house with a sequence of yards, should the official etiquette be followed to the letter, ushering in a guest would indeed be a time-consuming matter. Because the passing of each gateway is a penetration into new depths of someone's privacy, "at each gateway the host must respectfully urge his guest in until they arrive at the door of the inner courtyard. The host excuses himself to enter first so that he may place the mats personally. As he comes out to show the guest in, the latter must repeatedly decline before capitulating." The procedure is as follows: "The host enters the doorway and turns to the right, and the guest enters and turns to the left. The host proceeds to the eastern stairway, while the guest proceeds to the west [the house-yard complex is therefore clearly oriented to the south]. If the guest, for some special reason, such as his inferior social rank, insists upon climbing the eastern stairway, the host must refuse in a most persistent manner; and then the guest may go back to his own side and be ready to ascend. In ascending the stairway the guest follows the host's moves [observe the longitudinal symmetry]; as the host lifts his right foot to ascend the eastern stairs, the guest lifts his left foot to ascend the western stairs."[36]

This horizontal division of the many courtyards is already rigid in assigning to each a different meaning; but the raised terraces exercise yet another tyranny. They dictate the path for movement, and the statements of their inviting stairways and prohibitive corners are firm and final. In the longitudinal symmetry of the idealized house plan there is also a division separating the front and the rear. This echoes the distinction between respect and intimacy in Chinese etiquette. The honored guest, or a messenger from the emperor for that matter, is received with the greatest respect in the hall facing the main courtyard, but the private quarters of the house where the family dwells is beyond, and only intimate guests and relatives may enter there. The dual quality of the house, as a setting for ceremony and as a home, is a most important characteristic of the house as an image of human relationship. It reaches its climax of sophistication in the eighteenth-century painting of the Grand Audience scene (plate 106) which shows officials at their proper stations in the foreground, and the rear quarters of the palace attended by eunuchs and palace personnel.

Theoretically, the number of courtyards one could have, and the accompanying sense of depth in privacy, was determined by one's status. The situation of a house in a *fang* (a square of houses with its own network of streets), as indicated in Han dynasty sources, was again determined by the status of the owner. However, instead of the seclusion in depth, it was the prominence of the location that denoted prestige within a *fang*. Houses with one, or only a few courtyards, opened to a side street or lane. More magnificent houses, therefore having more courtyards, opened to larger streets and main thoroughfares.[37] The entire city was made of groups of *fang* in which houses of all sizes were organized. In the case of the capital city, the emperor occupied the central and largest house-yard complex, thereby dominating the walled-in town and, symbolically, the nation. Such regularity as that seen in the Sui-T'ang capital of Ch'ang-an, or in the greatest and last of this tradition, Peking, was by no means always a rule or a fact since the earliest times. The development has been a long process and the eventual synthesis incorporates elements from many sources. Indeed, when the powerful and the rich vied for splendor, as during Emperor Jen-tsung's reign (1023–63) in the Sung dynasty, these classical codes of propriety were shattered by the building of magnificent and luxurious structures clustered in the capital city of Pien.[38] As the cities rose and fell on the terrain of China, the Chinese house-yard and its "graduated privacy" developed an interesting and organic pattern of city life, in which the separation of houses was as clear as the sense of sharing in a community was enduring. Describing a spring night in such a city, the T'ang dynasty poet *Li Po* (701–762) sang:

> *From whose home comes this music of a jade flute?*
> *Borne by the spring breeze, it fills the city of Lo-yang!*[39]

Sitting in his hall and facing his courtyard to the south, the Chinese sees himself, in an idealized manner of course, not at all fixed in the center of his world, but longingly looking out beyond his walls. In almost every aspect his attitude is different from that of his Indian counterpart. He focuses his eyes on the ground instead of heaven; he is the originator of knowledge and not the seeker of enlightenment who makes the eternal pilgrimage from the periphery toward the center. The Chinese organizes his basic cell in order to organize the world around it. His immediate world, measurable, controllable, is forever encroaching on the Unknown. His kingdom is the Central Kingdom. In adverse times his sphere can be reduced to a hibernating spore, inactive and defensive but still organic (plate 104). Inside his walls he regulates human relationships to achieve internal harmony, to him the highest goal on earth.[40] As the society became complex and the relationships between men more refined, new architecture was created which further clarified human positions and their movements in space.

Recent excavations along the Yellow River basin, where ancient sites of China proper are concentrated, show early awareness of spatial orientation. It is interesting that the first noticeable fenestration of the neolithic pit-dwellings, from Pan-p'o-ts'un in Shensi to An-yang in Honan, faces the south. Although it is hard to determine from this that traditional orientation has its roots in that remote past, it is good sense for a house in the Northern Hemisphere to take advantage of the position of the sun in this manner. The same cannot be said of the tombs; their orientation has to have other meaning. Statistics (if any meaning can be attached to them at the present preliminary stage of investigation) show a rather random orientation with perhaps a majority of tombs facing the north. From various sites in Honan, some two thousand tombs have been excavated and sketched. They fall into three succeeding periods and appear to develop steadily toward greater consciousness of order and orientation. While the earliest tombs have only one approach

—and that from no particular direction—as a second approach appears, the later tombs suggest a strong north-south alignment. The better constructed and more elaborately furnished ones of the third period (Late Shang, twelfth-eleventh centuries B.C.), known as the royal tombs, acquired, in addition to the north-south axis, a new east-west one; but the latter never gained equal status. In the plan and section of the Great Tomb at Wu-kwan Ts'un near An-yang, man is seen again in this early design as at the center of the six-sided world (plates 108, 109). Underneath the center of the main pit is a *yao-k'eng* (or "waist pit") enclosing the sixth side. *Yao-k'eng*, common in Shang tombs, contained a sacrificed dog or sometimes a low-ranking official who was "underburied" as if to support the lord and to give the pit a bottom separating it from the infinite depth of earth below.[41] In tomb construction, it is clear that, if the position of the sun has any significance at all, it must be a symbolic one and therefore is not to be interpreted in a practical sense. The Shang concern with the dead and the elaborate ritual of ancestral worship, as witnessed by the magnificent ceremonial vessels and oracle bones, was also behind an equally complicated burial rite. It may be possible that the early, seemingly random, orientation indicates a more primitive attitude of attributing significance to all directions, one of which was chosen in relation to a special situation. But when such rites became professionally codified by the high priests or diviners who figured prominently in Shang dynasty court life, a more rigid orientation emerged as that preferred for the royal status.

The magical meaning of orientation never died. In the beginning of the Han dynasty, in the third century B.C., Hsiao Ho is said to have oriented the rituals for the Wei-yang Palace to the north; an orientation considered unorthodox. Whatever was the case, historians for generations resorted to the alleged practice of magic as an explanation. They reasoned that as an extraordinary measure Hsiao Ho had to do this to contain certain unfavorable forces by a practice called *ya-sheng*.[42] The whole attitude should sound familiar to us, for we know that in the Indian tradition when black magic is practiced the right-hand circumambulation pattern is abandoned for a left-hand one. The codification and elaboration of primitive rites may be responsible for the Chinese traditional orientation and, indirectly, for the later development of longitudinal symmetry. If the neolithic houses and Shang tombs were affected first, experiments along the same lines probably were carried out next in the capitals of princeling states during the late Chou Period (plate 114). The perfect city plan had to wait until after its nucleus, the palace, adjusted itself to this concept of order.

Han dynasty's Ch'ang-an was a makeshift capital (plate 113). Enclosing two pleasure palaces from the conquered Ch'in house, the new city was not a rectangular one; it lacked both the northwest and southeast corners because of irregular terrain. The irregular shape has inspired the speculation that it conformed to the shape of the northern and southern "Dippers" ("*Pei-tou*" and "*Nan-tou*"), and the city has come to be known as Tou-ch'eng (The City of the Dippers). Such ideas probably were never in the mind of the designer, who had to expand the city and to throw a wall quickly around the usable palaces after the sack of the Ch'in capital. It doubtless seemed better to have a larger city with missing corners than a rigid small one; and, in addition, the two palaces were alongside each other, making a central axis potentially impossible. This was in the early years of the new dynasty while military campaigns in many areas of the country were still going on.[43]

One prominent feature of Han palaces, well documented in literature and evidenced by archaeological remains, is the high and steep terrace, an image well preserved in traditional paintings depicting the Han palaces.[44] The terrace is often made by shaping the top of a natural hill such as the Dragon Head Hill for the Wei-yang Palace. With so much natural terrain involved, it is difficult to expect the Han designer to organize more than the palace. Moreover, capital cities are like royal jewels; they survive re-settings. Thus, the Han dynasty Ch'ang-an cannot be considered as a classical city plan.

Preserved in the *Book of Rites* is a "Code Book of Works" (*K'ao-kung Chi*). The Han dynasty scholars may have edited the work and left their mark on it, but it could not have been a completely new fabrication. In this work a rather idealized plan of a city is given: "The capital city is a rectangle of nine square *li*. On each side of the wall there are three gates... The Altar of Ancestors is to the left (east), and that of Earth, right (west). The court is held in front, and marketing is done in the rear," forming a Chinese mandala of nine squares with man in the center.[45] After the great turmoil of the so-called Six Dynasties (220–589), when India's Buddhism, sponsored by many foreign rulers, developed roots in Chinese soil, and when China was united once again in the Sui dynasty toward the end of the sixth century, the new ruler (of mixed ancestry) picked a site southeast of the Han city and laid a bold new plan for its capital city, Ta-hsing. This plan combined Chinese classical ideals with Central Asian experiences.[46]

On the northern end of the central axis, the palace was built first, followed by the administrative city to its south giving it an added sense of depth. The capital city in turn enveloped the earlier administrative city and provided an approach the length of nine *fang* to its southern gate, the Gate of the Red Bird. As the palace backed against the northern wall, the design provided two market places, one left and one right. If it deviated from the ancient canons in many ways, it set new standards for both its size (5.8 x 5.28 miles) and its rigidity (eleven north-south streets and fourteen east-west streets, the former an odd number to provide a north-south axis). Later in T'ang times (618–906), it developed into a great cosmopolitan city known to many corners of the world, and inspired Japanese copies, Nara in 710 (approximately 2.5 x 3 miles), and Kyoto in 794 (3 x 3.5 miles).[47] As the great capital of Ta-hsing was taking shape villages were leveled, avenues laid out, and rows of trees were planted. According to legend there was one great old locust tree that was not in line. It had been held over from the old landscape because, underneath it, the architect-general had often sat to watch the progress of construction, and a special order from the emperor in honor of his meritorious official spared it from being felled.[48] Thus, except for this tree, the total superimposition of man's order on natural terrain was complete.

The imperial tombs of Han are monumental stepped pyramids that have caused some scholars to speculate on their relationship with the Mesopotamian West;[49] but they are reminiscent of the terraces so dear to the Han people. Underground construction of Han tombs, for example under the burial mound at Wang-tu in Shantung, utilized sophisticated arches of manufactured brick voussoirs to form a system of subterranean chambers.[50] Before such recent excavations, both the true arch and the corbeled were known through the famous Han example at Ying-ch'eng-tzu in Manchuria.[51] In the late sixth and early seventh centuries, a magnificent stone bridge of beautifully shaped low arch with auxiliary arches on each end was built by a mason named Li Ch'un in Chao-hsien (plate 116). A later imitation of the bridge was constructed nearby, and other examples of arched bridges, five or six of them, are still about.[52] However, a tradition using that technique for halls or palaces had not developed. It remained outside the *t'u-mu* system of superstructure.

China, like India, had an open back door to the nomad land of the northwest. The mobile tribesmen of the region were for centuries the carriers of inventions, institutions, and ideas. Coming to the Chinese scene, Buddhism adapted itself to the Chinese secular architectural complex and the Buddhist image was installed as the central figure. Terms such as *ssu*, *tien*, and *kung*, meaning administrative office, audience hall, and palace, were adapted to mean temples and shrines. Preserved on the carving of a tympanum of Ta-yen T'a (rebuilt in the early eighth century) is a detailed picture of a Chinese hall housing a Buddhist group (plate 115; *cf.* also plate 106). Here, the dizzy height of the Han dynasty palace terrace gave way to the comfortable elevation of the platform that dominated the central courtyard. The pedestal, known by a perfect Buddhist term, *shü-mi* seat, symbolizing Mount Meru, later became commonly used for both secular and religious buildings. Similarly, Chinese vocabulary worked its way into the Buddhist composition. On the lower part of the pedestal for Yakushi-Nyorai (eighth century), the Buddha of Medicine, are carved the four Chinese animal symbols at the corresponding cardinal points.

One new addition to the vocabulary gives evidence of Indian influence: the central vertical axis. The fabulous *Ming T'ang* of Empress Wu, which we know only from record, was built in 688 and featured an enormous central shaft of tremendous height. Also from literary sources, it seems that the metal column erected in 694, known as the T'ien-shu (the Heavenly Pillar), was even more obviously derivative. When the *Ming T'ang* was changed back to a secular palace hall in 739, the central shaft was properly removed.[53] In the Yakushiji Pagoda at Nara, such a central pillar can still be seen (plate 119). The theme may also be expressed in void, an imagined stairway to heaven, as found in the Ta-yen T'a (plates 117, 118). The section illustrates an ancient formula of composing a square pagoda, whereas its famous exterior is much later and actually of Ming (1368–1644) date. The pagoda should be read as five vertical elements instead of four: the more important central one, the "void," and the four solid masonry piers defining it. In the pagoda of the Upper Temple of Kuang-sheng Ssu, the exciting and dramatic experience of climbing the stairway to heaven is heightened by novel construction. The climber

39

ascending that dark void has to reach backward at the end of each flight of stairs for the beginning of the next, because the narrow space does not permit a landing (plate 120, also compare plate 53). Along the masonry wall are small niches for grasping or for resting a candle.[54] In the central "solid" type, the drama of the vertical theme comes to an almost horrifying revelation in the late-tenth-century wooden structure of the Hall of Kuan-yin in Tu-lo Ssu of Chi-hsien in Hopeh. The circumambulating believer climbs the stairs to meet the eleven-headed god face to face (plates 121–123).[55]

Again in the preserved Buddhist monuments we can approximate the evolution of the structural technique that has become the hallmark of Chinese wooden architecture. Known as *tou-kung*, this bracketing system was responsible both for relieving the wall of its weight-bearing function and for the graceful overhang of the eaves. As a module, its composition provided meaningful rhythm. From the ninth-century hall of Fo-kuang Ssu at Wu-t'ai in Shansi (plates 124, 125) to the eleventh-century pagoda of Fo-kung Ssu at Ying *hsien* (plate 127), we see the large, powerful *tou-kung* system become complicated and delicate. There are "over sixty" different formulas used in constructing this later building, the tallest wooden structure extant.[56] The history of later Chinese architectural construction was basically an evolution of the *tou-kung*. As indicated by preserved Han reliefs and models, the *tou-kung* was at first primitive and functional. During classical T'ang, it developed a powerful elegance. Its degenerated decorative status began after the fifteenth century, decidedly changing the visual effect of the building. The organic structure, with a reason for each interlocking support and cantilever, provided every bay of an older building with distinct individuality. Over each bay it assigned a section of the gently curving eaves that was different from the next. From one soaring corner to the other, the curve traveled along a predetermined path to its destination. Good reason was everywhere: in the heftier proportions of the diameter of the column, in its height, and in the carefully calculated inclination of the two end columns toward the center. A firm and strong sense of stability was the result of such a dynamic equilibrium. Contrasting this with other buildings (plates 105, 126, 140), we immediately notice a different attitude in the architecture of the later periods. There is a monotonous progression across the building from one end to another, strengthening the eave line between uplifting ends

40

over identical bays. The columns, tall and straight, make up a forest of indifferent verticals suggesting no direction of movement or relationship to the whole.

All five basic roof types had matured by Han times (plate 134). Memory of the past made the later builders assign the simple and dignified *ssu-o* ("Four Slopes"), Type *III*, for the main buildings on the longitudinal axis. Types *I* and *II*, having two ends blocked, are naturally used either for doorways or for minor buildings, whereas Type *IV*, opening to all four sides without discrimination, sits over the structure at the crossings of the plan. The more elegant *chiu-chi* ("Nine Spines"), Type *V*, less severe than the simpler Type *III*, graces the most important entrances. Serving the front and the rear, a Type *III* roof, formal, ceremonial, and masculine, is raised over Tai-ho Tien, the Audience Hall in the Peking palace group, while behind it Pao-ho Tien was under a Type *V* roof, refined, beautiful, and feminine (plates 106, 136).[57]

In the Chinese architectural tradition, so overwhelmingly secular in nature, there is nevertheless a whole family of buildings serving as a station where communication between man and Heaven takes place. For this significant function these buildings are outside, or rather beyond, the consideration of longitudinal symmetry, and are given a central plan which stresses a vertical sense of continuity. The late Chou and Han records mention the emperor's "Ming T'ang" where he performed religious ceremonies for the state. The ritual required the emperor to move his position in a circular movement around the center to complete a revolution in the course of one year.[58] Although, quite obviously, there could be no intention of following this impossible ritual to the letter, rulers of China for the sake of prestige nevertheless ordered "authentic" Ming T'ang to be built. There is no trace of any early Ming T'ang left and no excavation will ever locate the enigmatic original. But the validity of the legendary structure with its logical central plan has inspired numerous later versions calculated to satisfy the ceremonial and emotional needs of the time. As we have noticed, Empress Wu, being a usurper, had her special need for an extraordinarily splendid one. A recent excavation located the site of a first-century version of the lost image; it was proposed to be the Ming T'ang and Pi-yung (a circular moat around the square plan) of another usurper, Wang Mang (reign 9–23 A.D.).[59] Its central plan is accentuated by a sequence of concentric circles and squares, as is expected (plates 129–130).

Furthermore, it duly acknowledges the four cardinal directions not only by orienting its four sides to them but also by relieving these sides with extensions called *pao-hsia*, attached buildings emphasizing the central meeting place of all three axes. A feeble echo of the Chinese solution to a religious building is discernible in the unique and probably tenth-century Mo-ni Tien, the Hall of the Talismanic Pearl, sitting on the axis of the Temple Lung-hsing Ssu in Cheng-ting, Hopeh (plate 131). Paying due deference to the sequence of courtyards on whose axis it sits, the hall comes close to forming a perfect square. Its four *pao-hsia* "attend" the hall on all four sides, accentuating the central square. Early pagodas of China sat on the axis of the courtyard of the temple but, apparently because of the Chinese preference for the ceremonial hall as the seat of the Buddha, they yielded that position; and in some examples twin pagodas—one on each side—served to enhance the longitudinal symmetry. Mo-ni Tien remains as a rare but brilliant memento of the Ming T'ang-Pi-yung type of religious architecture.[60]

Keeping in mind both the secular buildings in horizontal sequences and the religious structures in concentric arrangements, we are now ready to read the *summa* of the Chinese City of Man in the architecture of Peking, a capital that has served six dynasties in six hundred years and has been modified and maintained continuously.

Superficially, the northern Inner City and the southern Outer City remind us of Ch'ang-an, which also extended its southern approach, and Lo-yang which had a southern region. Against this city of innumerable smaller walled-in courtyards, against its warp and woof of streets, a core of structures stands out more meaningfully in the orderly design: the Forbidden City and its long avenue of approach from the south with all the gates and yards enhancing each significant stage of procession (plates 132, 135). Unlike a temple which as the house of God can only be read by man from the outside in, the city of man is to be read both ways: the resident begins from the center, the stranger from the outside gate. Many experiences of this architectural space are preserved in records. Emperor Ch'ien-lung was pictured receiving Amursana, the Eleuthian Chief at Wu Men, the Gate of the Noonday Sun (plate 140).[61] The new candidates for Civil Service murmur their thanks to its gates and walls from outside (plate 139).[62] Therefore, to understand this design as the man in his city understands it, one begins with the central group, immediately grasping the whole composition and with full knowledge and control expanding his view farther and farther out (plates 132, 137, 138).

The *San-tien* (three halls: T'ai-ho, Chung-ho, and Pao-ho) occupy an I-shaped platform of three tiers. Again in terms of threes, they are in the central courtyard, dividing the palace city into three parts (plate 135). They are the ceremonial center of the royal house, and therefore symbolically of the nation as well. Behind the *San-tien* is the private courtyard of the emperor's household, with a group of three buildings in similar composition dominating that courtyard. In each group the central square building takes a Type *IV* roof, indicating a meeting point of the axes. From here on the world of man is a sequence of rectangular courtyards defined by walls and with graduated privacy. The Palace City is twice enclosed by city walls: first, by those of the Forbidden City with its elegant corner towers; and second by those of the city proper, austere, high, and protective. Then, still defining the sense of privacy, far beyond the city walls of Peking is the Great Wall of China. Outside of this, the "barbarians," or the "outsiders," dwell (plate 141).[63]

The height of the palace platform is nothing to compare with the steep terrace of the Han Palace; but leading to this climax is the long southern avenue whose length must be read as height. No matter how the natural terrain of China is formed, one always goes *up* to Peking (plate 136).[64]

The Chinese doorway (*men*, meaning much more than an opening and indeed an architectural complex in itself) relieves the continuous wall surface by exaggerating the void it creates. Indicating a particular depth along the axis of approach, each doorway gives meaning to the courtyard behind it. The practice of illustrating a Chinese hall with a frontal view, as if it were a Renaissance building introduced by its façade, is most misleading. The Chinese hall, considered singularly, is façadeless. But seen within the house-courtyard composition, it indeed has a façade: the superimposed image of all the doorways leading up to it. T'ai-ho Tien therefore is the climax after the sequence of nine important doorways. The emperor's Audience Hall is therefore "high," and we shall see how the height of Heaven is expressed.

In the Temple of Heaven complex, the Son of Heaven (representing all men), having descended to the basic ground level, turns around and faces *north* to perform the ceremony at this site. He offers his prayers on the day of the winter solstice, on the

43

yuan-ch'iu, the Circular Mount,[65] again of three tiers, commonly known as the Altar of Heaven. Although the white balustrades and the three-tier elevation are familiar, it is surprising to notice that the magnificent roof of yellow glazed tiles of T'ai-ho Tien is missing. Then we realize at once that this circular structure with a central plan does not belong to any courtyard, but is simply situated under heaven and on earth. On this altar man has no privacy from heaven, and the roof is removed as if it were a hat from his head. There is a mute message in the rectangular plan with its northern end rounded off. The traditional idea of *tien-yuan ti-fang* (heaven round and earth square) is here a vertical volume sitting squarely on earth and terminating in the firmament of heaven. The Altar, the small intermediate building, and the Hall of Annual Prayers (Ch'i-nien Tien, popularly known as the Temple of Heaven) are therefore the humble efforts of man to arrange on the horizontal axis elements that should rise in succession one above the other, with the necessary gateways to heaven in between. A divisional wall separating north and south symbolically separates above from below. Significantly it is in a semi-circular shape and therefore may be interpreted as a semi-spherical dome which the passage to the Temple must penetrate. The blue glazed tiles roofing the Temple are the roof of the entire composition—the azure sky (plates 145–147, 151–152).

The intermediate small building, the Huang-ch'iung-yü (the Imperial Firmament) at one time housed the tablets representing various gods and ancestors of the royal house.[66] It is the intermediary station between earth and heaven, just as the ancestors and the gods are perhaps the links between man and the mysterious energy of nature. In the ceiling of this small building, the square motif of earth is transformed into the circular motif of heaven as it progresses to the center (plate 149). The building is walled on all three sides except the entrance from the south, and the journey north is blocked; for from here, the way leads heavenward. The Temple of Heaven also has a domed ceiling inside this unusual three-tier roof construction. But here the circular motif in the middle rises above the dome leaving an "eye" in the ceiling similar to that of the Pantheon in Rome. Man's physical passage in the ceremony ends here, underneath it. He looks up and spiritually soars through the opening (plate 150).

On returning from such a trip to heaven, we can better understand man's world on earth. In his rectangular courtyard of

44

the T'ai-ho Tien, there is an unnatural sense of eternity, for the unchanging scene of worldly awe is maintained by eliminating all vegetation; there is no tree in that courtyard. But the Temple of Heaven compound is shaded by the enduring color of evergreens. A further illustration of the meaning of the square and the circle is the imperial Chinese tomb of the Ming dynasty, which has a circular mound to cover the burial chamber, even though the offering hall complex has a plan similar to the palace. Round earthen mounds are plentiful in the countryside of North China today. The circular world of Eternity is, after all, not a forbidden world, but man walks into it from his rectangular world only as he dies (plates 110, 111, 148).

The circular symbol as a notion of heavenly supervision is also invited into the hall of man in the form of a ceiling motif (plate 143). Directly above the throne of the Audience Hall, over the ruler of man, heaven hovers above its son.[67]

Some decorative motifs of Chinese architecture may never be positively identified. Beginning as early as representations in Han art, two finials rise from each end of the ridge of the roof. Existing examples, all dating from the Buddhist period, are clearly makara motifs superimposed over that early form (plate 142), known as *ch'ih-wei* in Chinese architecture.[68] Literary sources give a crowded scene of animal symbolism in buildings even before Han; dragons, animals, and birds lurk everywhere.[69] Here in the Grand Audience Hall of T'ai-ho Tien, the dragon looks down from the ceiling, and the makara motifs on either end of the ridge of the roof, like quotation marks bracketing a statement, isolate the roof as a mantle of heaven—its corners still airborne—dropping weightlessly down over the domain of man.

4   OUTSIDE THE SQUARE AND INSIDE THE CIRCLE:

GARDEN, THE REALM OF THE IMMORTALS

The unnatural shape of the city defines the area within, and at the same time gives meaning to the world outside the square. The equally unnatural order, *li*, (social norms and ceremonial rites created by man to govern his behavior and emotions) is operational only when it has the four walls as its reference of relevancy. That which is "outside the square (*fang-wai*)" would be outside his concern, once declared Confucius, the master of *li*, and this quotation is significantly in the Taoist classic, *Chuang-tzu*, for a different set of values rules that realm.[70] Designed with the basic concept of *tien-yüan ti-fang*, (heaven round, earth square), the Chinese mandala, as it radiates from the center, is a series of alternating and concentric circles and squares beginning and ending either with the square (order and knowledge of man), or the circle (chaos and truth of Nature), recalling such classical designs as the Han and the Six Dynasties mirrors with the immortals depicted in this twilight area and particularly the plan of the traditional Ming T'ang Pi-yung (plates 129, 130). It seems that in this sense of "graduated worldliness," man's intellectual order and nature's ways gradually change guard. The realm outside each square but inside the next larger circle may be conveniently called *t'ien-jen-chih-chi*, between Heaven and Man. In this eternally negative space, between reason and untarnished emotion, between the correctness of the straight line and the effortlessness of the curve, between the measurable and the romantic infinity, lies the Chinese garden which is between architecture and landscape painting.

A particularly good illustration of this sequential relationship is the imperial garden known as The Three Seas, a free form of water outside the Palace Courtyard but inside the Forbidden City. Introduced further into the rigidly correct central courtyard of straight lines is the disciplined but nevertheless meandering river that enters from the west and goes out to the east, causing five marble bridges to be built so the rituals can go on (plates 135, 144).[71] After this "dress" occasion for the formal meeting of nature and man, water resumes its free form again.

When man leaves this courtyard and enters his garden, thus away from organized society, he is not the social man who has to be myopic to eternal values so that he may function well in immediate situations, nor is he the biological man who is constantly becoming and is responsible for reproduction. He is, instead, the eternal man of Chinese landscape painting and poetry whose growth, adolescence and obligations for reproduction are either behind him or are not his concern. His physical being has been idealized to become a means to an intellectual end. Thus a gifted youth as an eternal man is allowed to mingle with his

46

elders in a *wen-hui*, literary gathering, and often an emperor may momentarily join his courtiers in the conversation of poetry, calligraphy and painting, annulling the rules of the rectangular society. Emperor Ming Huang of the T'ang dynasty went so far as to call his minister Chang Chiu-ling "Commander-in-chief of the literary world" (*Wen-t'an Yuan-shuai*), ruling over the group of which the emperor himself was a member.[72] Seeking companionship in a different manner, a lone mortal poet may transcend time in this realm of art, writing poems to echo similar experiences of ages past.

Entering the garden, frequently by a circular gate, one meets irregular forms and curvilinear movements (plates 153–159). Winding paths with awkward surfaces are calculated inefficiency. The "organization man" unwinds as he twists and turns, following nature's way along the garden path. Canons for garden architecture differ fundamentally from those for the palace. In constructing a palace the largest and most valuable timber was prized since at least late Chou times (eighth-third centuries B.C.).[73] But in constructing a garden the "worthless" waste material should be ingeniously employed.[74] There is also a new relationship between man and his architecture. Instead of following a set of rituals prescribed for it, as in the case of the palace, man participates in the design of his own garden and has the satisfaction of self-expression. Again unlike the palace, a garden may never be considered finished, and indeed is passed on from one owner to another much in the same way as a painting scroll, acquiring more colophons along the way and serving as a symposium through time.[75] Thus, any specific garden design is but a flickering of the changing scene.

This simple and innocent yearning to free oneself from one set of values in order to repair to another is obscured in the history of Chinese gardens—a history full of melodramatic attempts to construct the most magnificent garden. Thus the story of Hui-tsung (1082–1135), the artistically inclined Emperor of Sung, who because of his insatiable urge to expand his rock garden, Ken-yü, wrecked the country's economy, need not blind us to the meaning of the garden. There are numerous individuals who saw "the universe in a grain of sand" and enjoyed their humble and small backyards (plates 160–161). The small garden of Ssu-ma Kuang, noted for its humbleness, is a good example from the same period.[76] Even more numerous are those artists who do not need a garden to visualize thousands of miles of landscape in a painting, or to conceal eons of the fantasy of life in the picture of an insect. In this respect the Chinese sage and his Indian counterpart have the same message for us: with superior mental power, one needs no "ferry boat" to reach "the other shore."

Perhaps behind the praises for this one aspect of the garden is a more meaningful message. From the design of the early tombs to the latter day palaces there was an evolution toward an abstract order motivated by a need of intellectual security. The development of the garden, as a counter-current and as an equally old aspiration, offered another security: the romantic return to Nature and a new sense of unity for the intellectual exile. With self-awareness he found a different Nature upon his return—one that needed the courtyard as a stepping stone and one that had been reorganized. Only a few decades after the city of Ch'ang-an was completed, the T'ang House began a pleasure garden to its north, the Ta-ming Kung (plate 113). Whatever the original reason for its construction, it later became the *de facto* court.[77] Of the six important Ch'ing dynasty emperors with whom we associate the palaces and gardens of Peking, only one, Ch'ien-lung, died in the city as he wintered there. The other five died in their gardens or detached palaces.[78] As the court buildings and particularly the offering shrines at imperial tombs suffered from neglect, man everywhere lived confidently paying only token respect to his "cosmic diagram" that had served its purpose in bringing him to maturity.

The orders we have examined in both Chinese and Indian tradition now belong to the past. But the need for an architectural reference to man's position in his universe and to his own independent and creative self is still with us. More than ever we need a symbolic transition to ferry us architecturally away from our world of organized action, yet without leaving it, so that we may cultivate our "eternal" nature. For this one valid aspect the Chinese garden—in contrast to the formal garden—remains an enduring vocabulary from the past. Here, inside the circle and outside the square, man's creative imagination is untrammeled by myopic considerations. As he creates, whether in art, science or philosophy, he is not God—although he momentarily enjoys the status of the immortals.

48

1. *"Ssu-shen (Four Deities) Tile,"* ink-rubbing, ca. 200 B.C.

2. *"The Translation of Buddha's Alms Bowl to Tushita Heaven,"* bas-relief, medallion from the Amarāvatī Stupa, ca. 150 A.D.

3. *Haystack, near Barābar Hills.*

4. *Brahminical rite on the shore of Dhanushkodi.*

5. *Capital of Aśokan Column, originally on top of monolithic shaft probably 50 feet high and surmounted by a Wheel of Law, Sārnāth, mid-third century B.C.*

6. *Religious dance at a market place in Bangalore.*

7. "Sūrya," bas-relief, vihara, Bhājā, first century B.C.

8. Vihara at Nālandā, founded fifth century.

9. "Indra," bas-relief, vihara, Bhājā, first century B.C.

10. Vihara (Monastery 51), Sanchi, founded ca. 200 B.C.

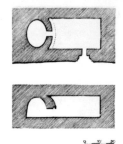
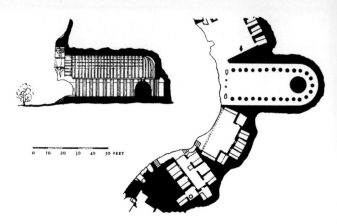

11. "Lomas Rishi" Cave, Barābar Hills, traditionally mid-third century B.C.: a) plan; b) section; c) entrance to inner room.

12. Chaitya Hall and Vihara, Bhājā. Section and plan.

13. Stupa with Image of Buddha, Chaitya Hall (Cave XXVI), Ajaṇta, sixth-seventh century.

14. "Lomas Rishi" Cave. Entrance.

15. *Ajaṇṭa Caves. General view.*

16. *Chaitya Hall, Bhājā, first century B.C.*

17. *Chaitya Hall, Kārlī, early second century.
Narthex.*

18. Chaitya Hall, Kārli. Nave with stupa.

19. Chaitya Hall, Kārli. Stupa.

20. *Partially preserved ancient path to Stupa II, Sanchi.*

21. *Stupa III, Sanchi, second to first century B.C.*

22. *Stupa II. Sanchi, late second century B.C.*

23. Stupa I, Sanchi. Eastern
    gateway, first century A.D.

24. Stupa I. Exterior. Original stupa of bricks begun in mid-third century B.C., enlarged from about 50 to
    140 feet in diameter and encased in stone in the second century B.C. when stairs and balustrades
    were added. Gates and sculptural details date from the first century B.C. to first century A.D.

25. Stupa I. Pradakṣiṇa path and stairs, upper level.

26. Stupa I. Pradakṣiṇa path.

27. Stupa I. Stairway near the southern gate.

28. Stupa of Barabudur, eighth century. Distant view.

29. Ruanweli Dagoba, Anurādhapura, ca. 150-90 B.C.
About 252 feet in diameter and 178 feet high, much
restored in the past 75 years.

30. Stupa of Barabudur. Aerial view.

31. *Stupa of Barabudur. General view.*

32. *Stupa of Barabudur. Plan.*

33. *Mandala of Avalokiteśvara, late nineteenth century. Tibetan.*

34. *A small stupa, Nāgārjunakoṇḍa, second-third century. Detail of base.*

85. *Stupa of Barabudur. Central stupa viewed through gateways.*

86. *Stupa of Barabudur. Corridor on a lower terrace.*

37. Stupa of Barabudur. Smaller stupas around the upper terrace.

38. Stupa of Barabudur. Smaller stupas around the upper terrace.

39. Stupa of Barabudur. Central stupa among the smaller stupas.

40. Stupa of Barabudur. Section.

41. Temple at Deogarh. Sculptural detail of lintel.

42. Temple at Deogarh, fifth-sixth century. General view.

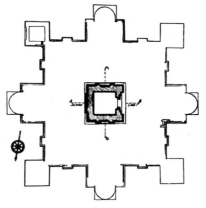

43. Temple at Deogarh. Plan.

44. *Pañcāyatana (five-shrine plan). An interpretation of the linear arrangement on the lintel of the temple at Deogarh.*

45. *Angkor Wāt, Cambodia, twelfth century. View looking west.*

46. *Mahābodhi Temple, Bodh Gayā, reconstructed nineteenth century. Original temple attributed to second century A.D.*

47. *Sūrya Temple, Koṇāraka, mid-thirteenth century. Detail of eastern doorway.*

48. *Lingarāja Temple, Bhubaneswar, eleventh-twelfth century. Sikhara.*

49. *Muktéśvara Temple, Bhubaneswar, tenth century. Sikhara.*

50. *Paraśurāmeśvara Temple, Bhubaneswar, seventh century.*

51. *Lingarāja Temple, Bhubaneswar. Sculptural detail,
showing the horizontal elements of the vertical
general effect.*

53. *Lingarāja Temple. Section and plan*

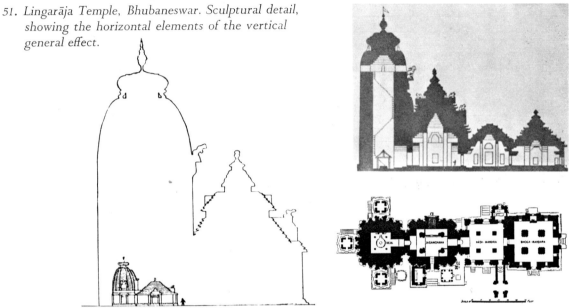

52. *Temples of Mukteśvara and Lingarāja drawn to the same scale. The Temple of Mukteśvara is placed
inside Lingarāja.*

54. *Lingarāja Temple. General view.*

55. *Durgā Temple, Aihole, sixth-seventh century. View from the apsidal end.*

56. *Durgā Temple. Pradakṣiṇā path.*

58. *Rajrajeśvara Temple, Tanjore, early eleventh century.*

57. *Viśvanātha Temple, Khajurāho, 1002-03. Exterior, approximately 90 feet long.*

60. *Kailāsanāth Temple, Elūra, late eighth century. Exterior.*

59. **Colossal Buddha, 175 feet high.**
Bāmiyān, Afghanistan,
fourth century.

61. *Kailāsanāth Temple.* Mandapa.

62. *Virūpākṣa Temple, Paṭṭadakal, dedicated 740.*

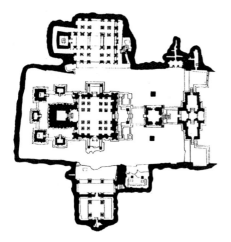

63. *Kailāsanāth Temple.* Plan of upper story.

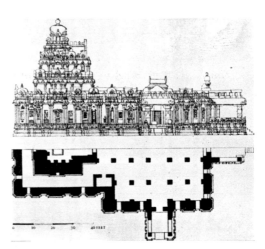

64. *Virūpākṣa Temple.* Half-plan and elevation.

65. Keśava Temple, Somnāthpur, 1268.

66. Vimala Temple, Mt. Ābū, eleventh century. Exterior.

67. Tejapāla Temple. Mt. Ābū, dedicated 1231. Main hall.

68. Vimala Temple. Main hall.

69. Sūrya Temple, Modhera, eleventh century.

70. Sūrya Temple. Ablution pool.

71. The Rock of the "Lomas Rishi" and other caves, Barābar Hills.

72. Bagh (Tiger) Gumpha, Udayagiri, Orissa, traditionally dated third century B.C.

73. *Sūrya Temple, "Black Pagoda," Koṇāraka, mid-thirteenth century. Exterior.*
74. *Sūrya Temple. Sculptural detail of musicians and mithuna couples.*

75. *Viṭṭhalasvāmin Temple, Vijayanagar, sixteenth century. Stone processional car.*

76. *The Great Temple Complex of Madurai, seventeenth century. Detail of interior corridor in front of the Mīnākṣi-devī Temple.*

77. *The Great Temple Complex of Madurai. The Golden Towers: Sundareśvar (Śiva),* **in center back-**ground, and *Mīnākṣi-devī (Pārvatī), in left foreground.*

78. The Great Temple Complex of Madurai. *View from the top of the southern gopura with Golden Lotus pool in the foreground.*

79. *Ritual procession in a southern temple.*

80. Śiva Temple, Rameshwaram, *seventeenth century. Procession corridor.*

81. *Makara lintel, Khmer, tenth century.*

82. *A T'ao-t'ieh mask design from a Chou dynasty ceremonial vessel, Fang-i, eleventh century B.C.*

83. *Angkor Wāt, Cambodia, twelfth century. Approach.*

84. Bayon, Angkor Thom, early thirteenth century. Detail of sculptured head.

85. Bayon, Angkor Thom. Serpent motif.

86. Bayon, Angkor Thom. General view.

87. Bayon, Angkor Thom. Detail of roof, serpent's scales motif.

88. Ruins of Angkor.

89. Stupa I, Sanchi. Sculptural detail of Eastern Gate.

90. The town of T'ung-lu, Chekiang.

91. *Walled-in courtyard. Mural from Tun-huang caves, eighth century.*

92. *House-yard complex. Stone engraving, probably third-fourth century, from a tomb at I-nan, Shantung.*

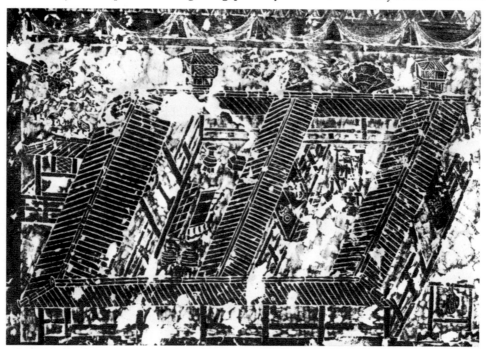

94. *Gate of Village House A, Chiao-hua (Pepper Flower) Village, Hopeh.*

93. *A one-courtyard town house, Peking.*

95. *Village House A. Inner room of the northern group, filled with winter sun.*

96. *Village House A. Doors to the rooms of the northern group.*

97. *Courtyard of Village House B. Paved walk leading to the northern rooms.*

98. Small courtyard known as a t'ien-ching (Heaven's Well), Chungking.

99. Houses, Sian.

100. Courtyards and roofs of the Forbidden City, Peking. T'ai-ho Tien is the highest; Chung-ho Tien and Pao-ho Tien, at left.

101. Stairs leading to T'ai-ho Tien, the Forbidden City, Peking.

102. Sian city wall, Ming and Ch'ing dynasties.

103. City wall, Feng-yang (hsing-ch'eng), Anhwei, fourteenth century.
Detail of corner, marble inlaid.

104. A small fort, Ninghsia.

105. T'ai-ho Tien, the Forbidden City, Peking.

106. "The Grand Audience on New Year's Day." Anonymous eighteenth-century painting.

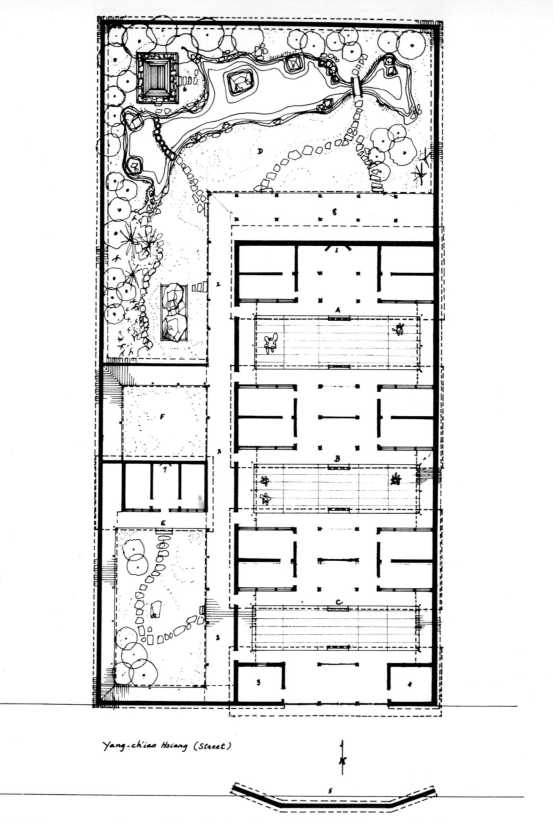

Yang-ch'iao Hsiang (Street)

107. *Plan of three-courtyard house with garden, based on the Wu family house in Foochow.*
A, B. C. Family courtyards. D. Garden. E. Family tutor's courtyard. F. Storage and service. 1. Family
shrine. 2. Service passageway. 3. Doorman's lodging. 4. Utility and refuse. 5. Pond. 6. Pavilion. 7. Tablet
of Confucius. 8. Loggia.

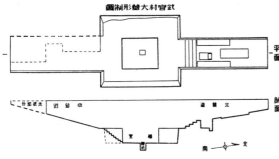

108. *The Great Tomb at Wu-kuan Ts'un, An-yang, Honan, twelfth-eleventh century B.C. Plan and section.*

109. *The Great Tomb at Wu-kuan Ts'un. Model.*

110. *Tomb of Emperor Shih-huang, Ch'in dynasty, third century B.C.*

111. *Tombs outside Chiao-hua Village, Hopeh.*

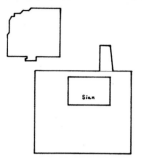

112. *The modern city of Sian as compared with the Han and the T'ang capital.*

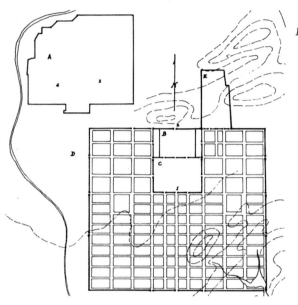

113. *Ch'ang-an of the Han and T'ang dynasties.*
A. Han dynasty Ch'ang-an, end of third
century B.C. B. The Imperial Palace of the Sui
and the T'ang dynasties. C. The Administrative
City. D. The capital of both the Sui dynasty,
called Ta-hsing Ch'eng, the City of Great
Prosperity, and the T'ang dynasty, called
Ch'ang-an, the Capital of Eternal Peace and
Security. E. Ta-ming Kung, the Pleasure
Palace of Great Luminosity: 1) Gate of the
Red Bird; 2) Gate of Hsüan-wu; 3) Site of Han
dynasty's Ch'ang-lo Palace; 4) Site of Han
dynasty's Wei-yang Palace.

114. *The Chao capital city, Han-tan, 386 B.C. Plan.*

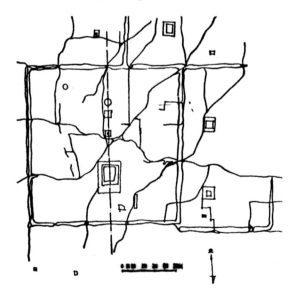

115. *Buddhist group. Stone engraving traditionally dated 704. From the tympanum of Ta-yen T'a, Tz'u-en Ssu, Sian.*

116. *An-chi Bridge, Chao-hsien, Hopeh, sixth-seventh century.*

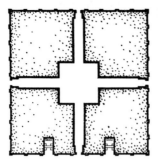

117. Ta-yen T'a, Sian, eighth century. Begun 652, rebuilt 704, surfaced with bricks, Ming dynasty. Plan.

118. Ta-yen T'a. Exterior.

119. Pagoda, Yakushiji, Nara, Japan, eighth century. Plan, half elevation and section.

120. Fei-hung (Winged Rainbow) Pagoda at the Upper Temple of Kuang-sheng Ssu, Chao-ch'eng, Shansi, sixteenth century. Inner stairway.

121. *Kuan-yin Ko (Hall of Kuan-yin), Tu-lo Ssu, 984. Statue of Kuan-yin.*

123. *Kuan-yin Ko. Plan and section.*

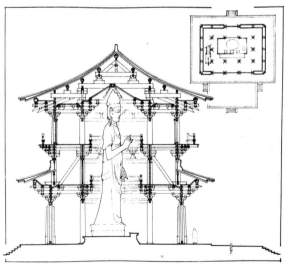

122. *Kuan-yin Ko. Exterior view.*

124. *Fo-kuang Ssu, Wu-t'ai, Shansi, 857. Main hall.*

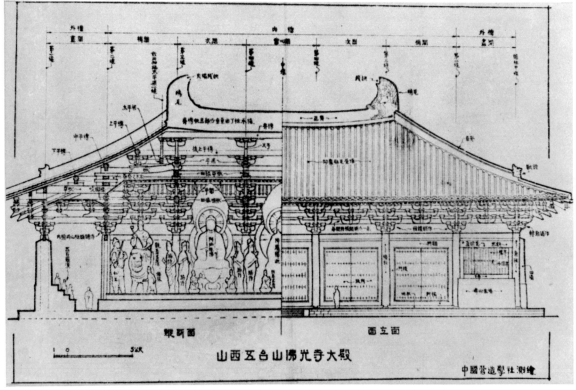

橫斷面　　　　　　西立面

山西五台山佛光寺大殿

中國營造學社測繪

125. *Fo-kuang Ssu. Section and elevation.*

126. Sheng-mu Tien, Chin Ts'u, T'ai-yuan, Shansi, early eleventh century.

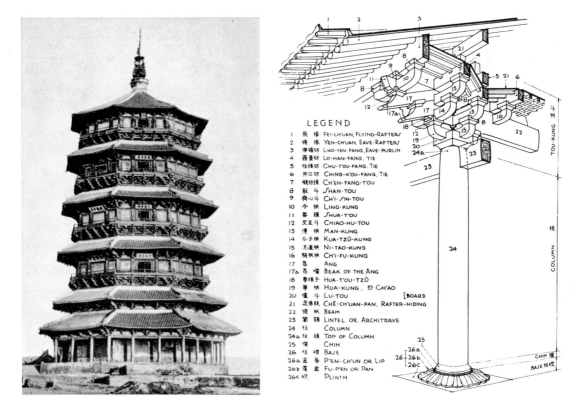

LEGEND

1 飛 椽 FEI-CH'UAN, FLYING-RAFTERS
2 檐 椽 YEN-CHUAN, EAVE-RAFTERS
3 撩檐枋 LIAO-YEN-FANG, EAVE-PURLIN
4 羅漢枋 LO-HAN-FANG, TIE
5 柱頭枋 CHU-T'OU-FANG, TIE
6 井口枋 CHING-K'OU-FANG, TIE
7 撐枋頭 CH'EN-FANG-T'OU
8 散 斗 SHAN-TOU
9 齊心斗 CH'I-SIN-TOU
10 令 栱 LING-KUNG
11 耍 頭 SHUA-T'OU
12 交互斗 CHIAO-HU-TOU
13 慢 栱 MAN-KUNG
14 瓜子栱 KUA-TZŬ-KUNG
15 泥道栱 NI-TAO-KUNG
16 騎栿栱 CH'I-FU-KUNG
17 昂 ANG
17a 昂 嘴 BEAK OF THE ANG
18 華頭子 HUA-T'OU-TZŬ
19 華 栱 HUA-KUNG, 抄 CH'AO
20 櫨 斗 LU-TOU   [BOARD
21 遮椽版 CHĒ-CH'UAN-PAN, RAFTER-HIDING
22 搨 栿 BEAM
23 闌 額 LINTEL OR ARCHITRAVE
24 柱 COLUMN
24a 柱 頭 TOP OF COLUMN
25 憤 CHIH
26 柱 礎 BASE
26a 盆 脣 P'EN-CH'UN OR LIP
26b 覆 盆 FU-P'EN OR PAN
26c 礩 PLINTH

TOU-KUNG

COLUMN

CHIH 憤

BASE 柱礎

127. Pagoda, Fo-kung Ssu, Ying-hsien, Shansi, 1056.
(Height 218 feet).

128. The tou-kung system. Diagram.

129. *Ming T'ang Pi-yung, Sian, early first century. A. Square terrace. B. Circular terrace (195 feet in diameter). C. Square terrace (673 feet north-south, 676 feet east-west, about 5 feet 4 inches above ground level). a. central buildings, b. corner buildings, c. well, d. gates, e. wall, and f. moat.*

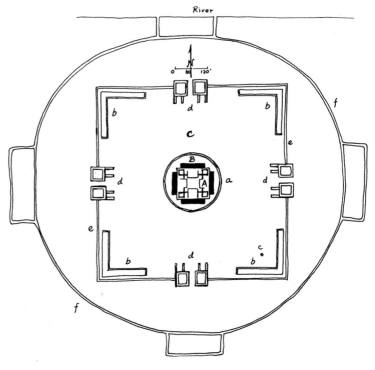

130. *Pi-yung, Peking, eighteenth century.*

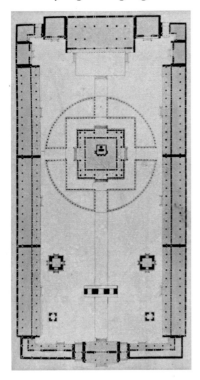

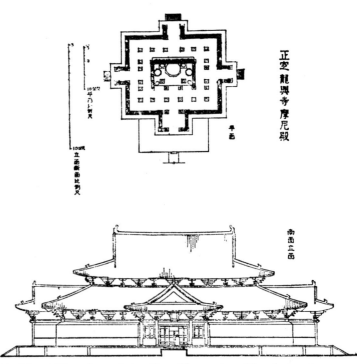

131. *Mo-ni Tien, Lung-hsing Ssu, Cheng-ting, Hopeh, tenth century. Plan and elevation.*

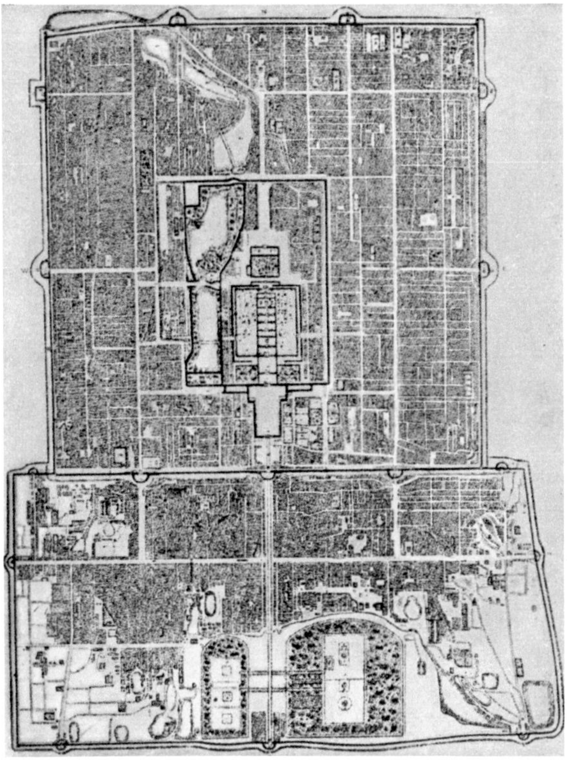

132. Map of Peking.

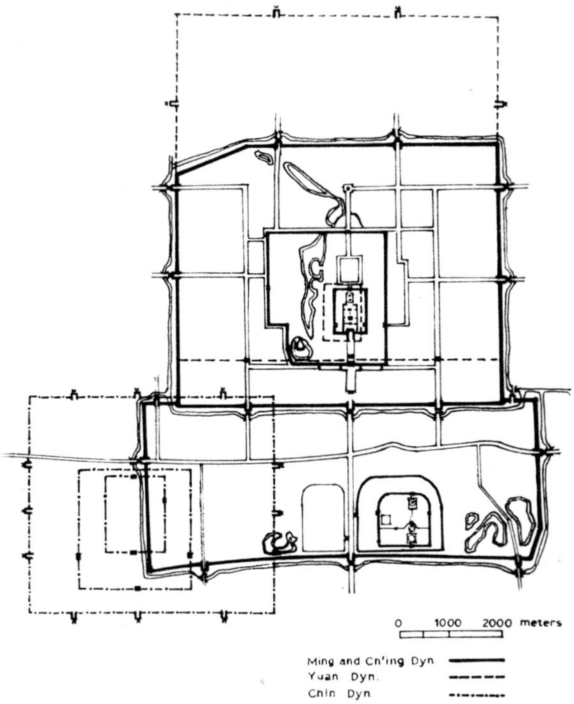

133. Superimposed plans of the Ming and Ch'ing dynasties' Peking, and the capitals of the Yuan and Chin dynasties.

0   1000   2000 meters

Ming and Ch'ing Dyn ━━━━━
Yuan Dyn. ━ ━ ━ ━
Chin Dyn. ━ · ━ · ━

I   II   III   IV   V

134. Typical roof types: I. Hsüan-shan (Hsia-liang-t'ou), roof overhangs gables. II. Ying-shan (Pu-hsia-liang-t'ou), no overhang. III. Ssu-o, four slopes. IV. Tsuan-chien, pinnacle. V. Chiu-chi, nine spines.

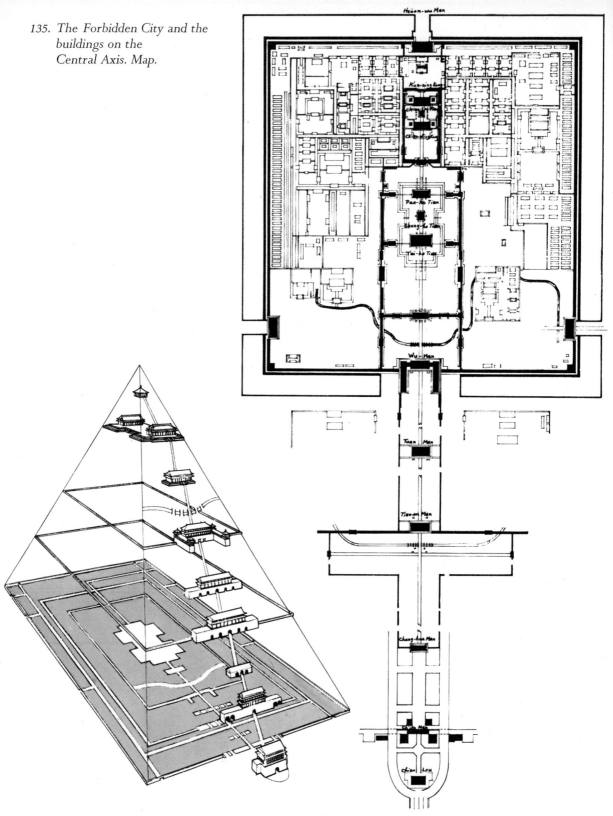

135. The Forbidden City and the buildings on the Central Axis. Map.

136. Plan of Peking interpreted as volume, with the front and rear courts of the palace superimposed, (shaded area).

137. *Air view of the Central Axis, buildings of the Forbidden City.*

138. *Air view of the Central Axis, southern section.*

139. Lin Ch'ing at the Wu Men (Gate of the Noonday Sun), thanking the Emperor for the Chin-shih Degree conferred upon him. Wood-block print, nineteenth century.

140. Emperor Ch'ien-lung receiving Amursana in 1754, in front of Wu Men. Engraving of 1774.

141. The Great Wall, near Nankou, Ming Dynasty.

142. *Shan-men (Temple Gate), Tu-lo Ssu, tenth century. Sculptural detail, ch'ih-wei.*

143. *T'ai-ho Tien, Forbidden City. Ceiling.*

144. *Nai-ching-shui Ch'iao (Bridges over the Inner River of Golden Water), the Forbidden City.*

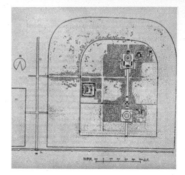

146. *The Temple of Heaven group. Plan.*

145. *The Temple of Heaven group, Peking, begun in the fourteenth century. Air view.*

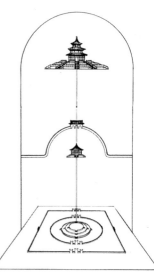

147. *The Temple of Heaven group. Plan interpreted as volume.*

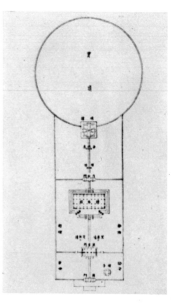

148. *Tomb of Emperor Yung-lo, Ch'ang-l'ing, Hopeh, early fifteenth century. Plan.*

149. *Huang-ch'iüng-yü. Temple of Heaven group*
(rebuilt in the nineteenth century). Ceiling.

150. *Ch'i-nien Tien (the Hall of Annual Prayers,*
known as the Temple of Heaven). Ceiling.

151. *Huang-ch'iüng-yü. Exterior.*

152. *Ch'i-nien Tien. Exterior (original building*
1540; last rebuilding 1890). Terrace base
approximately 300 feet in diameter; building
about 90 feet in diameter and 120 feet high.

153. *Garden Gate, Ts'ang-lang T'ing, Soochow. (Rebuilt in the nineteenth century.)*

154. *Entrance of Cho-cheng Yuan, probably sixteenth century, Soochow.*

155. *Liu-pei T'ing (The Pavilion of the Floating Cups), Nai-hai, the Forbidden City.*

156. *Bridge, Hsien Yuan, Mu-tu, near Soochow, 1828.*

157. *Shan-mien Tien, I-ho Yuan (the New Summer Palace), Peking.*

158. *Paved path and wall with ornamental windows, near Lo-shou T'ang, I-ho Yuan.*

159. *The Great Stones in Shih-tzu Lin (Lion's Grove), Soochow, (originally part of Temple, 1342).*

160. *Rocks at Yenling Yeyuan, Cheshire, Connecticut.*

161. *Stone composition, Ming Lake, Yenling Yeyuan.*

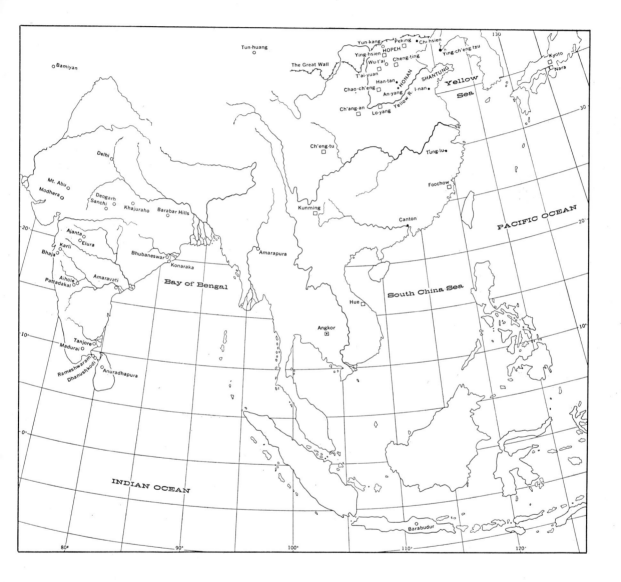

Tun-huang
○
Bamiyan
○

Yun-kang Peking • Chi-hsien
□ ○
Ying-hsien □ Cheng-ting Ying-ch'eng-tzu
The Great Wall HOPEH •
Wu-t'ai □ Kyoto
T'ai-yuan □ □ Nara
Chao-ch'eng Han-tan • HONAN SHANTUNG Yellow
□ An-yang • Yellow R. I-nan • Sea
Ch'ang-an Lo-yang □ •
□ □

Delhi
○

Mt. Abu Ch'eng-tu
○ □

Modhera ○ Tung-lu •

Deogarh
Sanchi ○ Khajuraho Foochow •
Barabar Hills ○
○

Ajanta ○ Kunming PACIFIC OCEAN
Elura □ Canton •
Karli ○
Bhaja ○ Bhubaneswar ○
Konaraka ○ Amarapura South China Sea
Aihole ○
Pattadakai ○ Amaravati Bay of Bengal

Hue •

Angkor
⊡

Tanjore ○
Madurai ○

Rameshwaram
Dhanushkodi ○ Anuradhapura

INDIAN OCEAN

Barabudur

NOTES

Chinese terms throughout this book are given in the Wade-Giles system, except in a few cases when the spelling in references is kept unchanged or the conventional romanization of place names is followed. For general readability and appearance, Sanskrit terms accepted by the *Merriam-Webster New International Dictionary*, 2nd edition, as anglicized are treated as such; but proper terms, such as names of classics, are given in traditional form with diacritic marks and in italics. Place names, if in use by the modern town, are given in the form used by the Indian railway systems and without marks. Others of interest only to archaeological studies are spelled with due respect to usage and the intention to achieve some internal consistency. Thus, stupa, sikhara, mandala, but *Mahābhārata* and *vāstupuruṣamaṇḍala;* Bhubaneswar, Madurai, but *Kārlī.*

1. Franklin Edgerton, "The Meaning of Sankhya and Yoga," *American Journal of Philology*, XLV, 1, 1924, p. 20.

2. The Chinese walled city is not to be confused with the idealized Indian village or city plan of the *Mānasāra Śilpaśāstra*, see P. K. Acharya, *Indian Architecture according to Mānasāra-Śilpaśāstra*, Oxford, 1927, pp. 40 ff., 143-145. They differ in every respect; see also note 40 and the discussion in chapter 3. On the other hand, the pattern of settlement in Chinese cities—such as extending to the outside of them along thoroughfares and, at the same time, failing to fill up the area inside the walls—demonstrates clearly that the plan has also been an idealized one.

3. One early reference is in the *Book of Rites (Li Chi*, "Chü-li"), p. 8. For English translation see James Legge, tr., the *Lî Kî*, p. 91. See also Fung Yu-lan, *A Short History of Chinese Philosophy*, New York, 1948, pp. 129–136; and by the same author, *A History of Chinese Philosophy*, Derk Bodde, tr., Princeton, 1953, II, pp. 19–30. Feng Yu-lang, *Chung-kuo Che-hsueh-shih*, Shanghai, 1933, pp. 200–209.

4. "Enduring Happiness (Ch'ang-lo)" and "Never to End (Wei-yang)" are also the names of the two early Han palaces. See discussion on Han architecture later. Ch'ang-lo was the name given by the new regime to the remodeled Hsing-lo Palace of the conquered Ch'in dynasty. Work was done between 202 and 200 B.C., according to *Chinese Histories: Shih Chi*, p. 0231-a; and *Han Shu*, p. 0296-c.

5. C. Sivaramamurti, *Amarāvati Sculptures in the Madras Government Museum, Bulletin of the Madras Government Museum*, Madras, 1956, p. 178. The reader must not be discouraged by the multitude of unfamiliar names. He should keep in mind that "plurality is the perishable" so that the sense of unity will be with him.

6. The definition for *yü-chou;* see note to "Yuan-tao," in *Huai-nan Tzu,*

p. 1b. The six-sided world is also mentioned in *Chuang Tzu*, I, 19a. I refer to the *ssu-pu-pei-yao* edition of both works.

7. For the invisible religious truth above all visual aids see also Zimmer, *Art*, I, p, 271. For an Aśokan column still standing see Rowland, *India*, Plates 8 and 9.

8. For Monastery 51 (plate 10), see M. Hamid, "Excavations at Sanchi," *Archaeological Survey of India, Annual Report*, 1936–37, Delhi, pp. 84–87; cf. also Mitra, *Sanchi*, pp. 49–50.

9. Julius Eggeling, tr., *The Śatapatha-Brāhmaṇa, The Sacred Books of the East*, XII, Oxford, 1882, p. 425, explanation and italics added. I am indebted to Professor Rulon Wells of Yale University for this reference.

10. My own experiences in several temples in China. For a procession of monks see J. Prip-Møller, *Chinese Buddhist Monasteries*, Oxford, 1937, Plate 187.

11. At one time most of these rock-cut chaityas perhaps had superstructures outside them. Traces are clearly visible at Kārlī and Kaṇherī. Like all religious architecture, the Buddhist caves functioned as places for social and court gatherings. These devotional festivities expressed also the splendor of the society that sponsored them. See Goetz, *India*, p. 55.

12. For a related situation, see note 14.

13. Important as it must have been as a Buddhist center, Sanchi was not mentioned in his journal by Hsüan Tsang, the Chinese pilgrim who traveled to India in 629–45. For a background of Sanchi, its pre-Gupta and Gupta eras, and a description of the monuments, see Sir John Marshall, *The Monuments of Sanchi*, 3 vols., Delhi, 1940. His *A Guide to Sanchi*, 3rd ed., Delhi, 1955, and D. Mitra, *Sanchi*, are concise handbooks. On the site of Stupa *I* stood the original stupa of bricks, about 50 feet in diameter and supposedly Aśokan in date. It was enlarged to about 140 feet in diameter and encased in stone in the second century B.C. Stairs and balustrades were also added at this time. Gates were finished in the early first century A.D. In view of the extensive reconstruction of all three monuments, my speculation as to the function and possible meaning of them is primarily based on the plans. The same principles are followed in my interpretations of other reconstructed temples.

14. Usually three times, "but in obedience to vows or by way of penance they will perform 7, 14, or even 108 *pradakshinas*." Marshall, *A Guide to Sanchi*, p. 37, footnote 1. The significance of the southern torana is discussed by Mitra, *Sanchi*, p. 14.

115

15. Buddhists from India, Ceylon, China, Burma, and various parts of Indonesia met here for a Waiçakha celebration in 1953. I am grateful to Dr. R. M. Soetjipto of the University of Indonesia for providing information about this event.

16. Scholars do not all agree as to the meaning and structural problems concerning weight, etc., of this monument. For this important monument a brief list of references should include: A. Foucher, "Notes d'Archéologie Bouddhique," *BEFEO*, IX, 1, Hanoi, 1909; N. J. Krom, *The Life of Buddha in the Stupa of Barabudur*, The Hague, 1926, and *Barabudur, Archaeological Description*, 2 vols., The Hague, 1927;

Paul Mus, *Barabudur*, Hanoi, 1935; Rowland, *India*, pp. 245-253; Zimmer, *Art*, I, pp. 298-312 (see p. 303 for the author's theories concerning structural weight).

17. Kramrisch, *Hindu Temple*, I, p. 7.

18. The "ferryman" and the "ferried" are frequent analogies in both Hindu and Buddhist scriptures. Instead of a ship or a boat, it may often be a raft, "*fa*" in Chinese literature. I quote from Woodward, *Sayings*:

> *Just as a ferryman boards his stout ship,*
> *With oars and steering-gear fully equipped,*
> *And ferries many other folk across—*
> *A shrewd, skilled pilot he, who knows his task.*—(p. 311)

And just as those crossed Ganga's stream and came safe to the further shore, so also, brethren, those brothers who, by the destruction of three bonds and by the wearing thin of lust, anger, and illusion, are Once-returners,—when they have once more come back to this world, they shall make an end of sorrow.—(pp. 313-314)

Also in the *Bhagavad Gītā* (iv, 36):

> *Even if thou art of sinners*
> *the worst sinner of all,*
> *Merely by the boat of knowledge all*
> *(the 'sea' of) evil shalt thou cross over.*

Franklin Edgerton, *Bhagavad Gītā*, 2 vols., Harvard, 1944, I, p. 51.

19. Cf. Fergusson, *History*, Plate 121 (p. 220), for the once ruinous conditions of this temple.

20. Not unlike the case of the chaitya. While Bhājā's octagonal and inward-leaning columns still remember their prototypes built with perishable materials, the sixteen-sided columns of Kārlī have straightened themselves up, more in keeping with stone. The image of the traditional chaitya opening, in the meantime, has been elevated to be above a pedestal-like ground floor (plates 11, 12, 13, 18).

21. Mitra, *Bhuvaneswar*, pp. 49-50, and K.C. Panigrahi, "Three Temple Inscriptions," *Orissa Historical Research Journal*, I, no. 2 (1952), pp. 1-9. W. W. Hunter, *Orissa*, London, 1872, p. 237, gave the date as "between 1099 and 1104." See also R. D. Banerji, *History of Orissa*, Calcutta, R. Chatterjee, 1931, I, pp. 343-344.

22. *Udāna*, v. 5. Translation is by Woodward (*Sayings*, p. 249). See also Mr. Woodward's other version in *The Minor Anthologies of the Pali Canon, Part II, Udāna: Verses of Uplift...*, Sacred Books of the Buddhists, VIII, London, 1935, p. 65.

116

23. The "Descent of the Ganges" was mentioned in many places. See *Mahābhārata*, III, 108-109; V, 188; *Bhāgavata Purāṇa*, IX, 9; *Viṣṇu Purāṇa*, II, 2, 8; and perhaps most important, *Rāmāyana*, I, 43. We must be clear-eyed about the two interruptions of the "Descent." As Ganga agreed to come down, and as the earth was not strong enough to withstand the downpour, Śiva was persuaded to receive her with his braided hair. Later, as Ganga flew merrily along, out of the god's hair, which obviously was the mountain's crown of vegetation, she swiped the platform of a holy sage. In both cases, we see the religious system's claim to authority. Śiva demonstrated his power not only by taking the impact

of the falling water, but also by holding Ganga prisoner in his hair until it was beyond any doubt that it depended entirely upon his will whether the world below might or might not have water. The priest had his say, too. When his platform was damaged, Jahnu, the rishi, "took the entire flood in his palm and sipped it off. Ganga disappeared again...," (to quote from the most colorful translation by C. Rajagopalachari, in *Rāmāyana*, Bombay, 1957, pp. 25-26). At the end of this second detour, Ganga finally came out of Jahnu's right ear. The roles of the god and the church as the receptacle and the agent for redistribution of heavenly grace must be behind the image of the mountain as religious monument. Compare Barabudur, a man-made holy mountain; Deogarh, mountain-temple; and Bayon, King-God as mountain. For the renewing of spiritual energy by going into disguise or hiding see *Mahābhārata*, III, 314, Again, for a very readable and faithful modern rendition, see C. Rajagopala-chari, *Mahābhārata*, Bombay, 1958, p. 129.

24. Fergusson, *History*, p. 143; see also p. 333, and Brown, *Indian*, p. 37.

25. N. Wu, "The Beginning, the Middle, and the End: The *T'ao-t'ieh*, the *Makara*, and the *Ch'ih-wei*," paper presented at Annual Meeting, College Art Association of America, Minneapolis, January, 1961.

26. Aubrey S. Trik, "Temple XXII at Copan," *Contributions to American Anthropology and History*, V, 27, Washington, 1939. A. Nawrath, *Indien und China*, Wien, 1938, Plate 62.

27. Kramrisch, *Hindu Temple*, I, p. 4.

28. Zimmer, *Art*, I, p. 283.

29. Fergusson, *History*, p. 347.

30. Known as Fu-nan and Chen-la, this general area of Southeast Asia was mentioned frequently in Chinese records. Indian customs and some-times names are discernible. Early entries in *Chinese Histories* include: *San Kuo Chih*, p. 1062-d; *Chin Shu*, p. 1337-c; *Nan Ch'i Shu*, p. 1758-c ff.; *Liang Shu*, p. 1839-c ff.; *Sui Shu*, p. 2534-a ff.; *Hsin T'ang Shu*, p. 4159-a ff.; and others. Chou Ta-kuan, who was sent to the Khmer country in 1296 by the Yüan emperor, and stayed there for about one year, wrote the *Chen-la Feng-tu-chi*, which is available in translations: Abel Rémusat, *Description des Voyages...*, Paris, 1819; and P. Pelliot, "Mémoires sur les Coutumes du Cambodge," *B.E.F.E.O.*, II, Hanoi, 1902. The latter was reissued as: *Oeuvres Posthumes de Paul Pelliot*, III, Paris, 1951. For further reading on Khmer culture and art see: H. Marchal *L'Architecture Comparée dans l'Inde et l'extrême-Orient*, Paris, 1944, pp. 118-167; G. Maspero, *Empire Khmer, histoire et documents*, Phnom, Penh, 1904; H. Parmentier, "The History of Khmer Architecture," *Eastern Art*, III, 1931, pp. 140-179; G. de Coral Rémusat, *L'Art Khmer, Les Grandes Etapes de son Evolution*, Paris, 1940; and Rowland, *India*, pp. 211-232.

31. See note 23.

32. For characteristics of Han terrace (*t'ai*), see Liang, *History*, pp. 21-22; Liu, "Han," pp. 132-133; Soper, *China*, pp. 219-220, and Plate 171.

33. *Chinese Histories: Shih Chi*, p. 0230-d ff.; *Han Shu*, 0457-a. Liu, "Han," pp. 147-148, attributes both palaces to Hsiao Ho.

34. For example, the T'ang capital of Ch'ang-an was demolished in 904, and

117

much of the building material was moved down the river to the new capital at Lo-yang. See *Chinese Histories, T'ang Shu*, p. 3148-a. For a Ch'ing dynasty example, see Liang, *History*, p. 105.

35. *Li Chi*, "Chü-li," pp. 1-2. Cf. Legge, The *Lî Kî*, "Khü Lî," 6.24-25, p. 65.

36. *Li Chi*, "Chü-li," p. 3. Again, cf. Legge, *ibid.*, 7.28-30, pp. 71-72.

37. Liu, "Han," pp. 130-133.

38. Liang, *History*, pp. 81-82.

39. *Chüan T'ang Shih*, VI, 90a, Shanghai, 1887.

40. "Ta-t'ung," the Great Unity or the Universal Peace, using Professor Bodde's terms. See Fung Yu-lan, *A History of Chinese Philosophy*, D. Bodde, tr., Princeton, 1953, II, p. 680 ff.; and Legge, The *Lî Kî*, "Lî Yun," pp. 364-366. Legge calls it The Grand Union. This ideal—certainly some aspects of it may be found in the Indian religious systems—is not in the Indian city architecture which stresses defense. See A. K. Coomaraswamy, "Early Indian Architecture, I. Cities and City-Gates, Etc.," *Eastern Art*, II, 1930, pp. 208-235; and E. B. Havell, *A Study of Indo-Aryan Civilisation*, London, 1915, pp. 1-32.

41. Recent findings on mainland China have been both plentiful and exciting. For a review and study (in English) of these publications up to 1960, see Chêng, Tê-k'un, *Archaeology in China*, I, II. For burials in Vol. II, see pp. 60-73, and pp. 225-226. For the excavations at An-yang, see Shih Chang-ju, *Hsiao-t'un*, "I. The Site, Fascicle 2: Architectural Remains," *Archaeologia Sinica*, Taipei, 1959. For a possible N-S axis, see pp. 63 ff.

42. *Chinese Histories: Shih Chi*, 0036-d; *Han Shu*, 0297-a. For a later example in the Six Dynasties, see *Nan Ch'i Shu*, 1756-a.

43. Returning from a military campaign, the Han emperor, Kao-tsu, was quite disturbed to find that under such difficult conditions Hsiao Ho had seen fit to build for him the magnificent Wei-yang Palace. Hsiao-Ho hastened to explain the importance of such a ritual structure and convinced the emperor of the symbolic and prestige value of the splendid architecture, especially after the prolonged period of unrest. See *Chinese Histories, Shih Chi*, 0297-a. The engineering and other technical problems of the buildings and the city seem to have been the responsibility of a Yang-ch'eng Yen; see *Chinese Histories, Han Shu*, 0343-b; and Liang, *History*, p. 22.

    For recent excavations on the Han site, see Wan Chung-shu, "Han Ch'ang-an-ch'eng k'ao-ku kung-tso ch'u-pu shou-huo," *K'ao-ku T'ung-hsün*, V, 1957; and a sequel, *ibid.*, IV, 1958. Cf. Liu, "Han," pp. 147-149, and I. Miyazaki, "Les Villes en Chine à l'Époque des Han," *To'ung Pao*, XLVIII, Livre 4-5, 1960, Leiden, 1960, pp. 1-18.

44. See note 32.

45. *Li Chi*, "Chou Li, K'ao-kung-chi," p. 129. The text could mean "measuring nine *li* on each side" but, comparing this measurement with excavated sites such as Han-Tan (plate 114), I find it too large to have been the practice.

46. For this section on T'ang dynasty Ch'ang-an, I am indebted to Professor Arthur F. Wright of Yale University. In addition to lending me his collection of Chinese publications on architecture, he put in my hands

118

his unpublished lecture, "Life and Death of a Cosmopolis: Ch'ang-an, 583-904," which he delivered at Princeton University, March, 1961.

47. Measurements in miles are from A. F. Wright's lecture and E. O. Reischauer, *Japan: Past and Present*, New York, 1951, pp. 23-25.

48. *T'ang Liang-ching Ch'eng-fang-k'ao*, I, 1b., in Hiraoka, ed., *T'ang Civilization Reference Series, No. 6*, Kyoto, Jimbunkagaku Kenkyūsho, 1956.

49. Liu, "Tombs," p. 116.

50. *Wang-tu Han-mu Pi-hua*, Peking Historical Museum, 1955, Plates 31-34, figures 7-10.

51. O. Mori, and H. Naito, *Ying-ch'eng-tzu, Archaeologia Orientalis*, IV, Tokyo and Kyoto, 1934.

52. S. C. Liang, "The Great Stone Bridge of Chao Hsien," *BSRCA*, V, 1, Peiping, 1934, pp. 1-31.

53. *Chinese Histories: T'ang Shu*, p. 3075-d; p. 3076-b (for T'ien-shu); p. 3081-b (the destruction of the T'ien-shu); p. 3085-a and p. 3159-a (the destruction of the Ming T'ang and the removal of the central shaft).

54. Whei-yin Lin and S. C. Liang, "A Brief Report of a Preliminary Investigation of the Ancient Architecture of the Upper Fen River Valley," *BSRCA*, V, 3, 1935, pp. 46-48, and fig. 10.

55. S. C. Liang, "Two Liao Structures of Tu-lo Ssu, Chi Hsien," *BSRCA*, III, 2, 1932, pp. 49-88.

56. S. C. Liang, "Chi Wu-t'ai-shan Fo-kuang-ssu Chien-chu," *BSRCA*, VII, 1, 1944, pp. 13-61, and his *Tsu-kuo-te Chien-chu*, Peking, 1954, pp. 14-15. Cf. Liang, *History*, pp. 108-109, counting "some thirty-odd types" of *tou-kung* (p. 109). In his *Tsu-kuo-te Chien-chu* the author gave the number as fifty-seven. But *Chung-kuo Chien-chu*, published in 1957, the latest on this problem, claimed "over sixty" (see captions at back of book for Plates 54-55, p. 4).

57. Liang, *History*, p. 32; *Ting Pao, Tun-tseng Liu* and *S. C. Liang*, "The Architecture of the Han Dynasty," *BSRCA*, V, 2, Peiping, 1934, p. 8. *Chung-kuo Chien-chu*, fig. 2. The buildings in the Rear Court, as indicated by their names, reflect the roof types. They are called Masculine Purity, Feminine Serenity, with the Union in between.

58. *Li Chi*, "Chou Li, K'ao-kung-chi," p. 130. For a very good and concise review of this complicated problem, see Soper, *China*, p. 212 ff. The posthumous publication of Professor William Edward Soothill, *The Hall of Light*, London, 1951, conveys the complexity of the matter.

59. According to T'ang Ching-yu, "Hsi-an hsi-chiao Han-tai-chien-chu i-chih fa-chueh pao-kao," *KKHP*, II, 1959, pp. 45-55. For other suggestions of its Ming T'ang-Pi-yung possibilities see articles by Hsü Tao-ling and Liu Chih-p'ing and references cited in *KKHP*, IV, 1959, pp. 193-196.

60. For a later version of this plan, see B. Melchers, *China*, Hagen, 1922, Plate 69, and Plan XVII; *Pei-ching Ku-chien-chu*, Plates 63-64.

61. *Suite des seize Estampes représentant les Conquêtes de l'Empereur de la Chine*, Paris, 1774, Plate 1. There is really no evidence that Amursana ever came to Peking in 1754. To the contrary, the Emperor arranged to meet him in Jehol. See *Ch'ing Shih-lu*, under Kao-tsung, nineteenth year, CCCCLXIX, seventh moon, pp. 6a-b, 10b ff.; CCCCLXXVI, 11b ff. It

is particularly interesting, therefore, that the court artists (said to be the four Catholic priests—Castiglione, Sichelbart, Attiret, and Salusti) should have the setting moved to in front of Wu Men where normally such ceremonies took place, while labeling the engraving: "L'Empereur Kien-Long, reçoit à Gé-Ho, les hommages…" See Liang, *History*, p. 160; and A. W. Hummel, ed. *Eminent Chinese of the Ch'ing Period*, Washington, 1943, for articles by Fang Chao-ying: "Amursana," and "Chao-hui." The meeting of the two was a significant fact in history, but the representation of it in front of Wu Men was an important fact in art history.

62. At the moment of this ceremony, Lin Ch'ing was technically a *kung-shih*. He was conferred the *chin-shih* degree shortly afterward when he passed two other examinations, the last, at the court. Before that time, his experience of Peking stopped at Wu Men where his trip up the pyramid was blocked as shown here. Lin Ch'ing, *Hung-hsüen-yin-yuan T'u-chi*, Yang-chou, 1847 edition, Vol. I, "Wu Men Shih-ho [Casting off the rough hemp clothing at Wu Men to become an official]."

63. The Manchus of the Ch'ing dynasty who were responsible for most of the extant palace buildings, and the Mongols of the Yuan dynasty upon whose "Great Capital of Yuan" the later dynasties built, and the Chin rulers of still earlier time, were all technically "barbarians," to the Chinese (Plate 133). They all utilized the Chinese concept of Ta-T'ung (see note 40) and the architecture of graduated privacy to advantage in their dealing with other barbarians. The term *yeh* [-*jen*], roughly translated as "barbarian", was simply the term used by those in the city to designate those outside of it. *Cf.* the term *yeh* in *tsai-yeh* (not holding court appointment, in the wilderness) and *tsai-ch'ao* (at the court).

64. The main room on the northern end of the family courtyard is known as the upper room (*shang-fang*). One goes up (*shang*) to it. Mountain and cloud motifs on stairways also help make this point clear (plate 101).

65. The exact manner in which the rituals were performed varied from time to time. For the practice in late Ch'ing dynasty, see *Ch'in-ting Ta Ch'ing hui-tien*, 1909 ed., Chapter XXXV, p. 1a ff. According to this, the emperor worships the Earth on the day of the summer solstice at the *fang-tse*, the "square swamp" (which is actually a square altar, but appropriately situated to the north of the city). He worships at the Temple of Heaven in the beginning of the year, in the spring. Records of this may be found repeatedly in the *Ch'ing Shih-lu*. It is interesting to note that while one emperor, Ch'ien-lung, spent three days purifying himself and then performed the rites at the Temple of Heaven, he sent representatives to conduct the ceremonies at his ancestral tombs (CCCCLXXVI, p. 11a). See also Shan Shih-yuan, "Source Materials for the Historical Study of the Architecture of the Ming Dynasty," *BSRCA*, V, 3, 1935, pp. 110-138.

66. Shan, "Source Material…," *op. cit.*, p. 120. Also, *Pei-ching Ku-chien-chu*, p. 12, and Liang Ssu-ch'eng, *Tsu-kuo-te Chien-chu*, Peking, 1954, p. 17.

67. Common in Buddhist temples, tombs, etc., of course with variety. For discussion on this and related problems see Soper, "'The Dome of Heaven' in Asia," *The Art Bulletin*, December, 1947, p. 227 ff.

68. B. Matsumoto, "Ch'ih-wei K'ao," *Tōhō Gakuhō*, XIII, 1, Kyoto, 1932, pp. 1-29.

69. A. Waley, *The Temple*, London, 1923. See "The Lung-Kuang Palace at Lu," pp. 95-97.

70. *Chuang Tzu, Ssu-pu-pei-yao* edition, Chapter III, pp. 10a-11a; *cf. ibid.*, Chapter I, p. 19a. For negative attitude toward the unknown outside, *cf.* p. 7 in Chapter I, *supra*.

71. Outside of T'ien-an Men, the Gate of Heavenly Peace, the same motif of river and bridges is repeated.

72. Beginning with the time of Confucius, examples are plentiful. For an outing of a mixed age group, highly approved by the master, see J. Legge, tr., *Confucian Analects, The Chinese Classics*, I, Oxford, 1893, pp. 248-249. The anecdote of Emperor Ming Huang was reported to be in *Yü-t'ang I-shih*. The original source, although cited frequently by standard references, is not available. I discussed another image of these concentric circles and squares in the Chinese society. See my "Toleration of the Eccentric," *Art News*, May, 1956. The Eccentric was recognized as "among us," and "inside us."

73. *Meng Tzu. Ssu-shu-wu-ching*, 9th ed., Vol. I, Shanghai, Shih-chieh Shu-chü, 1936, p. 14. The size of the timber must have had much to do in determining the height and the intercolumniation, and thus the size of the palace building.

74. Kan Tuo, "Yüan-yeh Shih-yü," *BSRCA*, II, 3, 1931, p. 8. (Notes on the Ming dynasty classic of garden architecture, Chi Ch'eng, *Yuan-yeh*.)

75. The Shih-tzu Lin, for instance, was originally part of a temple, 1342. Some forty years later, the painter Ni Tsan painted a picture of it. The layout was copied in the Palace in Jehol during the Ch'ing dynasty and named Wen Yuan. Similarly, Ts'ang-lang T'ing, Soochow, was a tenth-century garden, a temple in the fourteenth-sixteenth centuries, enlarged in 1697 and rebuilt as a garden in 1873. The Hsieh-ch'ü Yuan of the New Summer Palace was begun in the fourteenth century as an informal garden. After some two hundred years of intermittent building activities, the area was made into a palace in 1702. The present plan dates back to 1750. After almost total destruction in 1860 and subsequent reconstruction in 1888, it again suffered extensive damage in the war of 1900.

76. Called "Tu-lo Yüan (Garden for Solitary Repose)," its smallness caused special mention by Li Ko-fei, also of Sung dynasty, in the latter's *Lo-yang Ming-yüan-chi*, Peking, 1955, pp. 10-11.

77. The site of Ta-ming Kung has been extensively excavated from March 1957 to May 1959. See *T'ang Ch'ang-an Ta-ming Kung*, Peking, 1959. [*Ta Ming Kung of The T'ang Capital Ch'ang An*, with an English abstract, edited by The Institute of Archaeology, Academia Sinica.]

78. Wang Wei pointed this out in his *Yuan-ming Yuan*, Peking, 1957, p. 3, note 1. K'ang-hsi died in Ch'ang-ch'un Yuan, Yung-cheng and Tao-kuang died in Yuan-ming Yuan, whereas Chia-ch'ing and Shien-feng died in the detached palace in Jehol.

BIBLIOGRAPHY

Today's student of architectural history should find the study of Chinese and Indian architecture refreshing and rich in opportunity. There is still a wealth of material to be investigated, as well as theories and conventions to be re-examined against the architectural remains. Through the greatly activated field work and intensive study of historical records in recent decades, one may hope to assemble much new information eventually to effect a better understanding of these two architectural traditions. In this fast-changing scene of scholarship our brief bibliography can only represent a sample of what has been helpful to this modest attempt at interpretation. Some basic references and sources of good illustrations are included. The reader will find several other important journals, current and discontinued, cited in the notes. Works mentioned by abbreviation in the text or in the notes are listed here with full reference.

INDIA
Abbreviations

Brown, *Indian* Brown, Percy, *Indian Architecture*, 2nd ed. Bombay [1st ed., 1942]. Vol. I. Buddhist and Hindu.

Coomaraswamy, Ananda K., *History of Indian and Indonesian Art*. Leipzig, Karl W. Hiersemann, 1927.

Fergusson, *History* Fergusson, James, *History of Indian and Eastern Architecture*. London, John Murray, 1899.

Frédéric, Louis, *Indian Temples and Sculpture*. London, Thames and Hudson, 1959.

Goetz, *India* Goetz, Hermann, *India, Five Thousand Years of Indian Art* in *Art of the World* Series. Baden-Baden, 1959.

Kramrisch, *Hindu Temple* Kramrisch, Stella, *The Hindu Temple*, 2 vols. University of Calcutta, 1946.

Mitra, *Bhubaneswar* Mitra, Debala, *Bhubaneswar*, Department of Archaeology, India, New Delhi, 1958.

Mitra, *Sanchi* Mitra, Debala, *Sanchi*, Department of Archaeology, India, New Delhi, 1957.

Rambach, Pierre and de Golish, Vitold, *The Golden Age of Indian Art, Vth-XIIIth Century*, London, Thames and Hudson, 1955.

Rowland, *India* Rowland, Benjamin, *The Art and Architecture of India*, 2nd ed. Middlesex, Penguin Books, 1959.

Spink, Walter, "On the Development of Early Buddhist Art in India," *Art Bulletin*, XL, 2, June, 1958, pp. 95-104.

Woodward, *Sayings* Woodward, F. L., tr., *Some Sayings of the Buddha According to the Pāli Canon*, Oxford University Press, 1925, Reissued in *World's Classics*, 1939 and 1942.

Zimmer, *Art* Zimmer, Heinrich, *The Art of Indian Asia*, ed., Campbell, J., 2 vols. Bollingen Series XXXIX. New York, 1955.

CHINA

Abbreviations

Chinese Histories	*Erh-shih-ssu-shih (The Twenty-four Histories)*, K'ai-ming edition, 9 vols. Shanghai (n.d.). (To conserve space, all references are made to this edition by page and the four horizontal registers indicated by a, b, c, and d from top to bottom.)
Chung-kuo Chien-chu	*Chung-kuo Chien-chu*, Peking, Wen-wu Ch'u-pan-she, 1957.
	Itō, Seizō, *Shina Kenchiku*, Tokyo, 1929.
Legge, *The Lî Kî*	Legge, James, tr., *The Lî-Kî, The Texts of Confucianism*, in *The Sacred Books of The East* Series. Müller, F. Max, ed. Oxford, 1885.
Li Chi	*Li Chi*, in the *Shih-san-ching* edition. Shanghai, Commercial Press (n.d.).
	Liang Ssu-Ch'eng (Ssu-ch'eng), Liu, Tun-tsêng, et al., *Chien-chu Shê-chi Ts'an-k'ao T'u Chi Portfolios for the Comparative Study of Architectural Details*, Li, Chieh, *Ying-tsao Fa-shih* (dated 1100), 4 vols., Shanghai, Commercial Press, 1954 ed.
Liang, *History*	Liang Ssu-ch'eng, *Chung-kuo Chien-chu-shih* [History of Chinese Architecture], Peking, 1954.
Liu, "Han"	Liu Tun-tseng, "Ta-chuang Shih Notes," [Portions on Han architecture], BSRCA, III-3, Peiping, 1932, pp. 129-171.
Liu, "Tombs"	Liu Tun-tseng, "Ta-chuang Shih Notes," [Portions on Han Royal Tombs], BSRCA, III-4, Peiping, 1932, pp. 111-122.
Péi-ching Ku-chien-chu	*Pei-ching Ku-chien-chu*, edited by Chien-chu-k'o-hsüeh, Yen-chiu-yuan, and Chien-chu-li-lun-chi-li-shih Yen-chiu-shih, Peking, Wen-wu Ch'u-pan-she, 1959.
Sirén, *Gardens*	Sirén, Osvald, *Gardens of China*. New York, Ronald Press, 1949.
	Sirén, Osvald, *History of Early Chinese Art*. Paris, 1926. Vol. III, *Architecture*.
Soper, *China*	Sickman, Laurence and Soper, Alexander, *The Art and Architecture of China*. Middlesex, Penguin Books, 1960.
	Soper, A. C., *The Evolution of Buddhist Architecture in Japan*. Princeton, 1942.
	Willetts, William, *Chinese Art*, Vol. II. Middlesex, Penguin Books, 1958, pp. 653-754.

Periodicals mentioned by abbreviations:

ASI, AR	*Archaeological Survey of India, Annual Reports*, Calcutta
AA	*Artibus Asiae*, Ascona, Switzerland
BEFEO	*Bulletin de l'Ecole Française d'Extrême-Orient*, Hanoi
BSRCA	*Bulletin of the Society for Research in Chinese Architecture*, Peiping
HJAS	*Harvard Journal of Asiatic Studies*, Harvard-Yenching Institute: Cambridge
KKHP	*Kao-kü Hsueh-pao*, Peking

INDEX

Numbers in regular roman type refer to text pages; *italic* figures refer to the plates.

ACKNOWLEDGMENTS

This essay has been developed from one of my Abby Aldrich Rockefeller Lectures on Oriental Art delivered in March, 1960, at Harvard University. Professor Lien-sheng Yang, Harvard University, and Professor Paul Mus, Collège de France and Yale University, have been kind enough to go over the present version. During the preparation of this book, my colleagues, Professors Arthur F. Wright, Vincent J. Scully, Jr., and Rulon Wells, advised me on specific points. I am deeply grateful to all these friends, and doubly so to Professor Wells who has been most generous with his time in double checking Sanskrit and Pali sources for me, and to Professor Scully who read both an early draft and the final copy.

Without important contributions by the pioneer scholars of eastern and southern Asian architecture, this present interpretive, and indeed at times speculative, essay could not have been contemplated. While accepting the responsibility for the many observations made here, I wish to acknowledge my indebtedness to the authors whose works are either cited in the notes or recommended in the bibliography. Their devoted labor has been in many ways the inspiration for this present work.

For my experiences in southeast Asia and a return visit to India in 1958-59 after a fourteen-year lapse, I should like to acknowledge my gratitude to Yale University for the Morse Fellowship I received, and to the American Council of Learned Societies for its fellowship award. Without the full cooperation of the museum curators, the officers in charge of archaeological monuments and excavations, and the priests and abbots of temples and monasteries in this vast area, serious study on this extensive journey in such a short time would have been impossible. To them, I give my most sincere thanks. I remember with great pleasure the days I spent with them and hope to visit them again, seeking an understanding of the monuments on a higher plateau.

In the study of Chinese architecture, I was benefited by the wealth of illustrative material left at Yale University by Dr. Liang Ssu-ch'eng. I hope over the great distance between us, I can reach him with this book carrying my thanks. To Time, Inc., I am grateful for the use of its rich photographic files under the direction of Miss Doris C. O'Neil. I want to thank Mr. Henry Luce, III, and Miss Ruth Fowler for permission to use several photographs from these files. Miss Ming-hsien Wu, Messrs. Thomas Kubota and Roy Mason, students of the Yale Architecture School, helped with the preparation of most of the drawings.

I welcome the opportunity to have this essay included in the Braziller series on the GREAT AGES OF WORLD ARCHITECTURE. For fitting the original manuscript into the present framework, I am grateful to the editors for their patient collaboration. To Mrs. Ashton Goddard, I give my thanks for performing cheerfully the tedious task of preparing the manuscript through some five rewritings in my effort to cut the original draft in half while still preserving a meaningful essay.

NELSON I. WU
Yenling Yeyuan
Cheshire, Connecticut

SOURCES OF ILLUSTRATIONS

Unless otherwise noted, photographs are the courtesy of the author.

Bosshard, Peking; Courtesy of Black Star Co., Inc., New York: 98

Bulletin of the Society for Research in Chinese Architecture, (III, 2): 142; (IV, 2): 131, 148; (V, 3): 120; (VII, 1): 125

Burke, James, *Time-Life*, New Delhi: 104

Chung-kuo Chien-chu (Peking, 1957): 91, 92, 110, 114, 115, 116, 121, 122, 124, 126, 134 (redrawn), 153, 156

Les Conquêtes de l'Empereur de la Chine, (Paris, 1774): 140

Department of Archaeology, New Delhi, India: 43, 53

Ebersole, R., *Black Pagoda*, University of Florida Press (Gainesville, 1957) : 53

Courtesy of the Government Museum, Madras, India: 2

Hsi-an Wen-wu Sheng-chi (Sian, 1959) : 112, 113 (maps redrawn), 118

K'ao-ku Hsüeh-pao, XII (Peking, 1951) : 108, 109; II (Peking, 1959) : 129 (redrawn)

Kessel, Dimitri, *Life Magazine*: 94, 95, 96, 97, 100, 105, 111, 137, 138, 144, 145, 150, 151, 152

Krom, N. J. and Erp, T. van, *Beschrijving van Barabudur* (The Hague, 1920): 30

Liang Ssu-ch'eng, Peking, 123, 128

Lin Ch'ing, *Hung-hsüeh-ying-yuan T'u-chi* (Yang-chou, 1847), Vol. I: 139

Melchers, B., *China* (Hagen, 1922): 130

Mydans, Carl, *Life Magazine*: 99, 102

National Palace Museum, T'aichung: 106

Needham, Wesley E., Hamden, Connecticut: 33

New China, Foreign Language Press (Peking, 1953): 149

Pei-ching Ku-chien-chu (Peking, 1959): 93, 101, 133, 146

Rambach, P. and De Golish, V., *The Golden Age of Indian Art, Vth-XIIIth Century*, Thames and Hudson, Ltd. (London, 1955): 52

Rowland, Benjamin, *The Art and Architecture of India*, Penguin Books, Ltd. (Middlesex, 1956): 12, 32, 40, 63, 64

Sekino, Tokyo Imperial University: 119

Sirén, Osvald, *A History of Early Chinese Art* (London, 1930): 127

Sirén, Osvald, *Gardens of China* (New York, 1949): 154, 155, 157, 158, 159

Courtesy of the Smithsonian Institute, Freer Gallery of Art, Washington, D.C.: 82

Tokyo Imperial University, 1902 (redrawn from map): 135

Courtesy of Yale University, Photograph Collection, Art Library, New Haven: 1, 117, 132, 141, 143

128

Printed in photogravure and letterpress by Joh. Enschedé en Zonen, Haarlem, The Netherlands. Set in Romulus with Spectrum display, both faces designed by Jan van Krimpen. Format by William and Caroline Harris.